This is for my mother, Irene Boyd. She raised me gently, taught me the rules of life and civility, and kept me humble. When I told her I was writing an autobiography, she said, "That's nice, dear. Who is it about?"

Acknowledgements

This book would not have been born without publisher Scott McIntyre nagging it into life, and it would not have survived infancy if editor Brian Scrivener had not been there to nourish its first attempts to crawl. Boundless thanks to Diane Scott, Wayne Smith and Craig Ferry of the *Vancouver Sun* systems department for guiding a slow and Luddite learner through the Macintosh Quadra 605 jungle, and to former *Sun* editor-in-chief Ian Haysom for insisting that I get the bloody spelling right. And special thanks to author and buddy Pete Loudon, for blazing the first written trail back to Anyox.

"I realize very well that the reader has no great need to know all this; but I need to tell them."

Jean Jacques Rousseau, *Les Confessions*

SPIRIT OF CHILDHOOD

VANCOUVER 1933

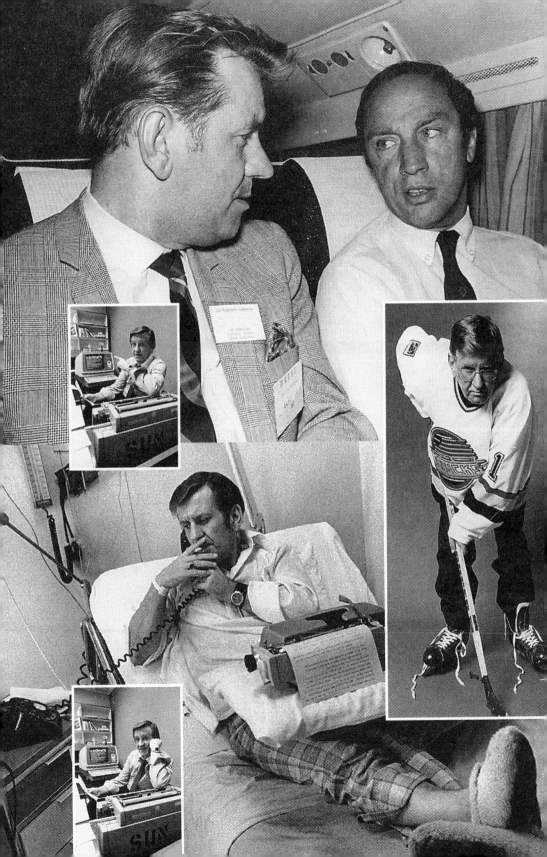

Before

When our number came up, we packed a few things and left the little mining town where I had been born.

It was the summer of 1935. I know this because my mother has told me many times. She and my father had been given plenty of notice by the company that the mine, and therefore the town, were closing down, that everyone would have to move out. In a company town, you don't argue with the company that has provided your entire living. It was not a brutal eviction order; nobody was given twenty-four hours to get out of town. Everyone who worked for The Company — that is, everyone in town — was given advance notice, and a departure schedule was drawn up to cover three months, factoring in the gradual closure of the mine operation, family considerations and southbound steamship schedules. Everyone was given a departure date. Ours was in the late summer.

I don't recall any excitement, sadness or particular happiness that we were leaving. Even now, my memories of the little mining town are sketchy . . . rusty, coppery soil, trees turned into gaunt white skeletons from the industrial smoke, heavy snow in the winter, the smell of skunk cabbage, the only nonhuman growth that flourished in the hostile air and soil.

I do recall quite clearly one stab of terror. It was departure day. My mother, father and I were on the upper deck of the Union Steamships vessel *Catella* and it was a very social moment, friends aboard to say goodbye, those departing chattering about the new life, the new riches, that we would find in Vancouver. The elders

1

had all heard how the street gutters in Vancouver ran shinily with silver dollars, that a man willing to work could have his choice of jobs at up to a dollar an hour. Everything but the cigarette trees and the lemonade springs of the popular song of the time.

The gaeity was cut short when the ship's captain blew a thunderous blast on his whistle to warn all visitors ashore. We were ten feet from the smokestack. I had never heard such a volume of noise and, terrified, I burrowed under my father's long overcoat, wailing. I didn't see the receding shores of the place where I was born; I had my head buried in the quiet darkness of my father's coat. I never saw the town again.

The boat trip south was pure bliss. The weather was balmy, the seas were calm. The air in the ship always seemed to smell of good soup. We had a stateroom and a steward, a little cockney, who treated us as family members. He taught me to sing "What Do We Do With a Drunken Sailor," the first drinking song I became familiar with. There would be others. I learned to anticipate meal times by the sound of the little xylophone played by the smartly uniformed page boy, whose job and clear voice and attitude I envied.

It was night time when we arrived in Vancouver. The harbour was beautifully lit up. I had never seen such lights.

We were met by my father's sister, Auntie Bella, her husband, Uncle Joe, and their boy, my cousin Bert. Auntie Bella was a tiny, twinkly dumpling of a woman with chattering false teeth, warm and merry eyes and an infectious laugh. Uncle Joe was tall and quiet, left gaunt and pain-racked by the gassing he had survived in France in the First World War. But he had an ironic sense of humour, enormous patience, and he always treated me wonderfully well, forever shaking hands with me in a formal manner so that he could slip a five-cent piece into my palm. Bert was about sixteen, tall and strapping, with friendly brown eyes. He became my second hero, after the page boy on the steamer.

While Auntie Bella clucked on about how wonderful it was to see us, Uncle Joe and Cousin Bert loaded us all into the family car, a four-door Essex, I believe. Cousin Bert let me have the window

in the plush back seat of the first real automobile I had ever been in.

As we drove up Kingsway, I was captivated to silence by the tall streetlights along the sidewalk. I had never seen such lights.

Cousin Bert, smiling at the wideness of my eyes, asked me, "What do you think of Vancouver, Cousin Dennis?"

I answered, "The moon on sticks."

I was five years old and I was enchanted. I had found wonderland.

My number came up on February 20, 1982. I know this is true because it says so on the damning blue document I still keep in my desk drawer.

The document is a Warrant for Arrest. It is addressed to "the peace officers in the Province of British Columbia." The file number is 03732.

It states that, "Whereas William Dennis BOYD (the 'accused') has been charged that on or about the 20th day of February, AD 1982 at the District of West Vancouver in the Province of British Columbia [because he] did unlawfully, while his ability to drive a motor vehicle was impaired by alcohol or a drug, drive a motor vehicle on Stevens Drive, contrary to the form of the statute in such case made and provided." And it went on to direct all those peace officers, in Her Majesty's name, "to forthwith arrest the accused and bring him before any Justice/Judge in and for the Province of British Columbia to be dealt with according to law."

I guess I might have quibbled with the wording. Actually, my crime wasn't so much driving a car on Stevens Drive, it was driving it *off* Stevens Drive when, pissed as a billygoat, I totally lost it, left the road and smashed into one of the very few vacant lots in the British Properties, coming to a stop just yards short of a steep drop into a gulch. But why equivocate? It was a fair cop, as they say in the Monty Python sketches. I was drunk and I was driving. I was damned lucky I didn't kill myself or someone else. I had spent the day, a Saturday, drinking a hole in a forty-ounce bottle of vodka. This was unusual in a couple of ways. Until a few days before that

Saturday in February, I had not had a drink in more than eight years. In 1973, out of work, broke and drinking heavily, I had been offered a new career, as sports editorialist at a successful Vancouver radio station, for more money than I had ever made in newspapering. In previous years, I had discovered I could write well enough to get by after a heavy night of drinking. But I knew I couldn't go on the air drunk. Additionally, I had met a lady who had had quite enough of drunks. So I quit — quit cold. Went white-knuckle, as they say.

The trouble with trying to control an alcohol problem by yourself is that you have no one but yourself to lean on. So eventually, and quite predictably, I toppled.

It seemed no big thing at the time. I just decided that, after almost nine years, I had the problem under control and could handle a drink or two. So I went to the liquor store and bought a bottle of nice tawny port and sipped it like a gentleman for a couple of days. And then I went back and bought another nice bottle of port and sipped that one away.

The third time I went back I got distracted. As I was passing down a row of shelves, a forty-ounce bottle of vodka rose up and jumped into my arms. It was a most amazing thing. So I took it home and scarfed it down like a pig. And the funny thing was, I had never been a vodka drinker. But I became one that day.

After my car stopped crashing through the little saplings in the vacant lot, the police came. They were most courteous. I immediately blurted out that I had been drinking. They examined me for wounds — a bloody nose and a bruised knee — cuffed me and drove me to the West Vancouver police station. Twice I blew well over the allowable limit. I was mug-shot and finger-printed and placed in the drunk tank. They released me at about 4 A.M. and I walked home. Hell, it was only five blocks. Back home, I finished off the vodka and did a quick review.

I had trashed a company car. I had a vague memory of bouncing off a couple of parked cars before I got onto Stevens Drive, so I could figure on additional charges. The other media would get

hold of the story and have some fun with it at my expense. My own paper would be obliged to report on it.

A feeling of crushing despair came over me. Somewhere, I had grown away from the enchanted little boy who had seen the moon on sticks. I was fifty-two years old and I was lost.

Chapter 1

I was born at 5 o'clock in the morning, June 18, 1930, in a bleak little British Columbia mining town that looked like a deep flesh wound.

The analogy is not exaggerated. The town died of copper glut when I was five years old.

The name of my birthplace is Anyox and I don't like to talk about it. Every time I tell someone where I was born, they get it all wrong. "Antioch?" they ask. And I say, in a rising-to-hysteria voice, "No, you stupid clot, it's not Antioch. And it isn't Any Eggs or Auntie Hocks. It's Anyox. Anne E. Ox! Is that so bloody difficult?"

And it really doesn't matter because Anyox isn't anything any more. It's a ghost town.

But Anyox was once a glittering, coppery jewel on the British Empire's crown, a rich producer of copper, located in a deeply-cut B.C. coastal fjord, Observatory Inlet, six hundred miles north of Vancouver, at the same latitude as Prince George. People who lived in Anyox simply refer to it as "up north," thus avoiding the aggravation of others' mispronunciation.

It was a one-industry company town, owned and operated by the Granby Mining Company. For more than twenty years the mine and smelter at Anyox were the biggest producers of copper ingots in the Empire. The ingots were stacked yards high on the shipping wharf when we left in 1935, the international price of copper having bottomed out disastrously during the Great Depression, forcing closure of the mine and the town and a life

that had been good for an itinerant population that reached as high as three thousand.

Only 480 of us were born there, in the small but efficient company hospital. If you were to return to the place of my birth today, you'd find not much but mine-tailings, heaps of slag, decayed buildings and fat bears.

My arrival in Anyox was not promising. My father, Duncan MacDougald Boyd, from Govan, Scotland, was in Victoria, attending a lodge convention. My mother, the former Irene Mabel Sager, from Sussex, England, was driven to the hospital on the morning of June 17, by family friend Jack Bell, in the borrowed company truck, one of only two vehicles in town that did not exclusively carry ore. By day, the truck collected the town's garbage. By night, after a good swabbing-down, it did extra duty for weddings, funerals and ambulance work. My mother sat in the passenger seat while Jack Bell drove.

I was a premature breech-birth, arriving — with the help of forceps — ass and elbows first, after a long and painful labour. My mother tells me that my head was misshapen, my body was covered with hair and the nurses cheerfully referred to me as my mother's "little toad." She was in hospital for two weeks following my difficult entry into the world.

Delivered by garbage truck. Arriving early and ass-backwards. Classified as amphibian. It wasn't exactly a Le Mans start in the human race.

Anyox was a grotesquely ugly place, made so by the products that sustained it — coke gases, sulphur fumes, accumulated slag and the copper deposits that gave the earth an orange tint. No trees grew near the townsite. The pre-mining old growth was killed by the poisonous emissions and stood like bleached, white pickets on the surrounding hills. The only life that flourished was the skunk cabbage, which inhaled the fumes with gusto, fattened and matched the mining operation stink for stink.

The town's chronicler, author Pete Loudon, claimed you could set the snow on fire with a match from the fine sulphur that fell on

it. Cyanide and sulphur killed the salmon-spawning beds in Falls and Hidden Creeks.

Sore throats were endemic, but for all its miserable physical shortcomings, Anyox supplied a good life for those who came there to work, primarily Northern English, Scots, Welsh and miscellaneous Europeans.

As a lifelong fiscal conservative, I find it amusing that I began my life under a system that was almost classic communism. Mother Granby owned everything — the mine, the smelter, the wharves, the housing, hospital, school, grocery store, movie house, dance hall plus the two miles of plank road, the truck, the superintendent's car, the two jitneys and the short rail line, cars and locomotives. Ninety-five cents of every dollar the company paid out in wages came back to the company in payment for services.

It is believed that Captain George Vancouver spent a night in Anyox harbour in 1793. He would have been impressed, perhaps intimidated, by its silent remoteness.

The site was prospected at the turn of the century. Granby came in during the mid-1920s searching for rumoured copper deposits. They found the copper, but in addition, they found enough gold and silver to pay for the mill, the smelter, the townsite and the widening of the harbour.

By 1929, 1,500 people lived in Anyox and 35 million pounds of copper had been shipped. The smelter, three furnaces burning twenty-four hours a day, exhaled continuous smoke through smokestacks twenty-two feet wide at the base, 150 feet high.

We lived in one of twenty-one comfortable cabins on the flats where the married men resided. Bachelors lived in the bunkhouse and visited the whorehouse out beyond the slag pile.

All the cabins had electric light, hot water and flush toilets. We had a wood-and-coal-burning stove, and my mother did the laundry by hand with a galvanized tub and a washboard.

The first spanking I ever received involved that stout kitchen stove, which my mother kept smart-looking with applications of stove black and silver polish.

She had left me one day in the care of an older boy, Jack Bell's son Kenny, while she ran errands. We decided to cook dinner and pulled out the first cupboard ingredients that came to hand. We tossed fistfuls of raw macaroni, mustard pickles and icing sugar onto the top of the stove, where it quickly congealed into stucco. The spanking I got left me with great respect for stoves.

My dad worked at the roundhouse, maintaining the locomotives and hopper cars that hauled the ore and slag. He made $2.50 a day and often worked a seven-day week, which allowed us to live well and send out for luxuries from Eaton's catalogue. My parents must have lived well because one of my prized possessions was an Ogden's Fine Cut tobacco can filled with the tiny white ivory horses that came tied around the neck of White Horse Scotch bottles.

There were weekly dances, picnics, sports days and boat trips to nearby Alice Arm. The law was maintained by a member of the B.C. Provincial Police. Anyone who made trouble was shipped out.

I have a few very clear memories of Anyox. While writing this book, I phoned my mother in Victoria and asked, "Did I have a yellow wicker baby buggy with big wheels, and did you used to take me in it when you and Dad played tennis on a wooden court?" She said I was bang-on and, "I don't know how you remember that. You couldn't have been more than two years old."

I have another memory, too, and a physical reminder of it.

On my last birthday in Anyox I got a terrific Tom Mix cowboy suit — hat, chaps, shirt, gun belt, bandana and two shiny cap pistols in holsters.

I swaggered up the plank sidewalk to terrorize a pair of neighbourhood sisters, a couple of years older. They didn't buy my act.

In fact, they disarmed me, tied me to their clothesline pole with my lariat and one of them walloped me over the head with one of my pistols, leaving a scar that remains to this day on my hairline.

Anyox didn't end with a whimper; it ended with a bang.

Suddenly, on a corporate decision made tens of thousands of miles away in Quebec and announced July 31, 1935, one thousand

9

men were jobless, 2,500 people were homeless and a $1.5 million payroll was discontinued.

It was a terrible blow to my parents. Both of them had grown up hard in Britain and their few years in Anyox had been the happiest of their lives.

My father, one of six children, was born on the banks of the Clyde River across from Glasgow. The Boyds (the original Celtic name was Buidhe, "the golden-haired one") had a colourful history in Scotland as insiders in the royal courts and political advisors behind the throne. One of our ancestors, William Boyd, was wounded and captured at the Battle of Culloden. Instead of being run through on the spot, as most of the surviving members of Bonnie Prince Charlie's Jacobite army were after the slaughter, Sir William was taken to London by the Duke of Cumberland (Stinking Willie, to loyal Scots) and publicly hanged.

None of the perks of royal association filtered down to my dad's family. He left school early to apprentice as a shipwright in the world-famous Harland Wolff shipyards and had the scars to prove it. He was still just a boy when a cable snapped under tension one day, whipsawed around, caught him across the shins and broke both his legs.

He, one of his brothers and all of his sisters left Scotland and came to Canada, my dad arriving in Anyox in 1923.

My mother was one of four Sager children born in the British midlands. Her father, William Hillary Sager (we are loosely related to Mt. Everest conqueror, Sir Edmund Hillary) was a sailor, a lovely man, but a rambler.

After working as a care-giver on the prairies and in Vancouver and Prince Rupert, my mother arrived in Anyox, joining one of her brothers, in 1927. Still a teenager, she worked as a waitress in the company-run cafe, where she met my father. "He came in one day and kept coming in. I had two boyfriends and I chose your dad," she told me. They married a year before I was born.

Fifty-nine years later she remembers life in Anyox with fondness. "We had a good life there. The rent on our house was $10 a

month and the light and water were free. Anything we wanted to buy, we sent to Vancouver for. There was really nothing we lacked. Food was fairly cheap. There was no fresh milk but we brought you up on KLIM, powdered milk that we bought in buckets and mixed with tap water. Everyone in the town was close, everybody looked out for everyone else. There was no crime at all.

"There were all kinds of activities, dances every week, the Elks' Ball, the Masons' Ball, real dress-up events and the July 1 picnic and sports day. Your dad played on one of the company soccer teams. Drinking never got out of hand because anyone who became a problem was usually sent out on the first boat. The friends we made in Anyox became our friends for life.

"It was a terrible shock when they announced they were closing the mine operation and the town down because the copper wasn't selling, it was just piling up on the dock. We knew the Depression was on in the rest of the country, but it hadn't been affecting us and we didn't know what to expect. We were pretty naive.

"The company did everything it could to make the move-out as easy as they could, plenty of advance warning. People packed up and left a few at a time and we had lots of going-away parties and we all promised to keep in touch. But we had no idea what we would be getting into when we decided to move to Vancouver.

"Considering that we lived in a little mining town, we all had very good furniture that we had shipped in. Most of us figured we could pick right up in Vancouver and that life wouldn't change much. So why bother taking the expense of shipping out our furniture? A couple of real sharp guys came up in a tugboat, hauling a couple of barges. They went around town telling everyone that there were plenty of jobs waiting for us in Vancouver. They convinced a lot of us to sell our furniture to them for ten cents on the dollar. People practically gave away pianos, dining room suites. There was just no way we were going to pay to have the kitchen stove shipped to Vancouver. We did pack up our good china and the household linen and we arrived in Vancouver with not much more than the clothes in our suitcases. Frankly, I was too young to

understand what the word we had been hearing, depression, really meant. And then we walked right into it, the moment we walked off the boat."

For me, a pale-faced five-year old, there was no wrench. I had no way of knowing how significantly my life was going to change. I was just going on a trip in a big boat and I would be meeting for the first time cousins I knew only from the letters that arrived from Vancouver.

I do have some vague, flash-imaged memories of Anyox. Drinking lemonade at the annual sports day and laughing myself to tears, watching grown-up men compete in the barrel race. Hearing my dad whistle to me as he came down the wooden sidewalk after work, swinging his lunch bucket. Using crayons and banging a cymbal in the preschool rhythm band. The enormous banks of sooty snow, reaching up to the eaves of our warm little house in the long, grey winter. Writing my first letter to Santa Claus and then, on the instructions of my mother, putting it into the roaring stove, where the rising heat would deliver it quickly in a dramatic shower of sparks to the North Pole which, I was convinced, was just over the mountain. Stealing potatoes from the pantry in front of our house and sharing them with older kids, who showed me how to roast "mickies" in a bonfire, and gingerly rubbing the blackened skins off the steaming treats.

And being taken out on the flats by an older girl and indoctrinated into the game of playing doctor. I don't remember her name, I have no idea what became of her, but I hope she took formal training to exploit her early obsession with proctology.

And so, in 1935, my parents packed up a few things — the china, the bedsheets, my dad's ritzy Rolls razor, the cloche hats my mother favoured, my one-eyed teddy-bear — and we left Anyox and came to Vancouver to get away from the effects of the Great Depression.

Out of the burning ship, into the icy ocean depths.

It wasn't entirely naivete; there simply were few alternatives.

Anyox was finished. The box score for the little town, from 1914 to 1935, read: 480 births, 320 deaths, 160 marriages.

There were other towns in B.C. we might have moved to, but we had relatives in Vancouver. They urged us to come and so, like desperate migrants from all over Canada, seeking a warmer climate and a new start, we came. And we walked into the middle of Canada's greatest agony, the period that my pal, author Barry Broadfoot, called in his book on the Depression, The Ten Lost Years.

It had started, worldwide, in 1929 and had been grinding Canadians into dry dust for six years before we felt the breadth and the unrelenting pain of it.

Between 1929 and 1933, the gross national expenditure of Canada (the consumer spending) dropped off by 42 per cent. By 1933, 30 per cent of the Canadian work force was unemployed. One Canadian in five depended on government relief to put a bowl of thin soup on the table.

The four western provinces, not as diversified as central Canada, suffered particularly. Just as Anyox failed because it depended on a single resource, so did the wheat-dependent prairie provinces. Wheat prices were the lowest in history, and, as if it were part of a devil's conspiracy, there was drought and crop failure. The total provincial income in Saskatchewan fell by 90 per cent in two years; 66 per cent of rural Saskatchewan people were on the dole or on the run. Nation-wide, the Canadian birth-rate fell, from 13.1 births per thousand in 1930, to 9.7 per thousand in 1937. Canadians were afraid to bring children into such a bleak, inhospitable world. There were outbreaks of scurvy in many Canadian small towns. Black despair was the common mood.

That was the national situation, the common mood, and it was no different in British Columbia. In 1930, Vancouver had seven thousand unemployed, Burnaby three hundred, North Vancouver two hundred and West Vancouver had twenty. And that was just the start.

By 1932, 34,000 people in Vancouver were on relief, with eight thousand in Burnaby and five thousand in North Vancouver city

and district similarly dependent. Relief payments were costing the city of Vancouver $250,000 monthly.

In 1932, the provincial government put Burnaby into receivership and it was run by a single commissioner until 1942. After hundreds of houses reverted to the municipalities for nonpayment of taxes, the city and district of North Vancouver suffered a similar fate in 1933: forty-five municipal employees, including the mayor, the manager and all the aldermen, were replaced by an appointed, one-man council.

There was no real estate market. Lumber mills closed. The canneries in Delta failed. Shipyards were padlocked. In Vancouver, grain shipments fell from 109 million bushels in 1932 to 68 million the following year.

Through most of it, the federal governments under R. B. Bennett and Mackenzie King tried to dump the grief onto the provinces and municipalities, urging them to create and maintain new public works projects. Burnaby, until it failed, paid married men between $2 and $3 a day to clear bush, the wage depending on the number of children they were feeding. Vancouver hired married men at $2 a day, single men at $1. When cash was short, the workers were often given a sack of groceries. Many men worked clearing bush on what would become the Barnet Highway. In West Vancouver, a squad of men cleared four thousand acres of slope, the beginning of the British Properties.

And it just got worse. In 1932, the Third Relief Act enacted by the Bennett government set up the despised work camps, supervised by the federal defence ministry. Primarily intended to keep single, itinerant men occupied, these camps paid 20 cents a day for labour seemingly designed to twist the back and break the spirit.

In 1932, the B.C. government decreed that relief payments be cut to $12.50 a month each for a husband and wife, and $2.50 a month for each child under the age of sixteen. Even the very wealthy felt the crunch. The Canadian Pacific Railway was repossessing so many mansions in Shaughnessy, under its mortgage plan, that the area became known as Poverty Heights. Servants

were fired as a first step to cost-cutting, many family mansions were turned into huge rooming houses. Property values skidded: The Glen Brae Estate, valued at $75,000 in 1920, sold in 1939 for $7,500.

Still the transients poured in from across Canada. Better to starve in a warm climate than in the wrenching winters of eastern Canada and the prairies. Hobo jungles developed on railway sidings and under the city's downtown bridges. Churches were hard-pressed to feed the hordes of men, in their cloth caps, in the soup lines. And of course there were the demonstrations and riots by the unemployed and the brutal reaction of the police. Mayor Gerry McGeer, elected in 1934, tried to provide jobs with the construction of Vancouver's new city hall, but he will be reviled until Judgement Day for reading the Riot Act to jobless men at Victory Square in 1935.

Vancouver historian Bettina Bradbury has written about this period in *The Vancouver Book*:

"Housewives struggled to use every little bit of food they could get, while at the same time trainloads of surplus fruit and excess milk were dumped into the Fraser River to prevent their swamping the market.

"Many families lost their homes and some rented them back from the municipalities. Others moved from rented house to rented house, either escaping or following evictions.

"The 'jungles' on False Creek and stretching up Burrard Inlet along Burnaby's waterfront and almost to Port Moody, included not only single men, but families as well. Flour sacks, carefully washed, began to adorn the home as curtains, pillow cases and were turned into clothes for children."

That was the big picture of the Great Depression but I don't remember it as such. It was too big and the colours too bleak for me to comprehend. I remember only the small pictures framed by the comfortable basement apartment we rented in the Victorian-style Avoca Apartments, at 1250 West Broadway, our first Vancouver home.

I never went hungry, I never went ragged and I never felt deprived. I was just beginning my first great discovery of Vancouver. I had things to do and places to ramble and every day was a bloody great adventure. My parents did my suffering for me and protected me. When I heard the word "relief" I thought it involved pills from the drugstore that cured something.

Like those neighbourhood kids whose dads had jobs, I saw my father head out every day. I thought he was going to work, not to seek work. I wondered why my mother spent so much time in the bigger apartments on the three floors above us, and why she was so tired at night, but I didn't think of it much.

I was a grown man, with kids of my own, before my mother dredged up the courage to tell me how she had "cheated" the relief system. She still doesn't like to talk about it, as if some authority might pinch her retroactively.

We received $27.50 a month as our relief allotment. There was a stipulation that no more than $9 a month of that relief money could be paid out in rent, and the outlay had to be accounted for. The Avoca Apartments were owned by an elderly widow named Mrs. Simmons. Maintaining the building was too much for her, so she cut a deal with my mother: she would return the $9 monthly rent in exchange for my mother serving as housekeeper. So, for nine precious bucks a month, my mother scrubbed floors, did the laundry and dusted, polished bannisters and cleaned dozens of windows. Her sweat put the odd pork chop on the table and sent me to school every day with hot cereal in my belly.

I recall her joy when she came back from the relief office with a shirt for me, a clean, second-hand shirt she had picked up for five cents. I hated it. It had a round collar, for crying out loud. It was a sissy shirt, a Lord Fauntleroy blouse. But I wore it. Our reactions were reversed the day she came home with a pair of high-topped boots, black lace-up clodhoppers with hooks and blaikies on the soles. I loved them: I could strike sparks by kicking the soles on the sidewalk. My mother hated them. She thought they would walk me straight into hooliganism.

My dad and I never had much communication. I guess it began during the Depression when I came to the unfair conclusion that he was a sad man. He wasn't really, he was just a terribly discouraged man. But, dammit, he was a man who tried.

To keep up the $27.50 we were receiving in relief benefits, he was required to take on any work that became available. One of those jobs was humping sacks of raw salt onto flatcars at the Vancouver Salt Works, on a railway siding just off Second Avenue.

It was tough work, but it was regarded as good work, and there was always a line of men outside the fences, waiting, vulture-like, to replace someone who couldn't hack it.

My dad developed boils on the back of his neck and on his right wrist. They were painful enough, but the raw salt, working into the sores, created agony and, eventually, blood-poisoning. Every day, the line running up his arm grew redder. Every night, my mother put poultices on the arm. And every day he went to work, toting those sacks of salt until he collapsed on the job from fever and poison. He was taken to the hospital and, of course, his job was gone the second he hit the ground.

One night, after dinner, he took me on the streetcar to a carnival down at Broadway and Cambie. I don't know where the money came from, but I rode the rides and stuffed myself with lemonade and cotton candy. I remember seeing him smiling reassurance at me as I clung like grim death to the pole on my rising, plunging merry-go-round horse.

I guess he spent everything he had because we walked home. I whined that I was tired so he carried me on his shoulders.

You couldn't have convinced me that night that life was anything but perfect. I had just had the greatest day in my life. I was riding home on Dunc Boyd's shoulders and I was on top of the world.

Chapter 2

By all the conclusions of modern sociology, I should have grown up gnarly and mean. Possibly sociopathic.

I certainly had reasons. I grew up during the worst depression and the most savage world war in the history of the human race. And according to the popular social mores of the nineties, that made me a victim, a condition that would have rationalized and excused any number of quirks and failings. But I am convinced that my parents, particularly my optimistic mother, shielded me from the long-term and deep-seated damage that might have accrued from surviving the thirties, that really were dirty.

So instead of growing up bitter and mean-spirited, I grew up alcoholic and journalistic, and all the mother's love in the world could not have prevented those inevitibilities. I think they were imprinted on my genes, in alcohol-based printer's ink.

This is a dreadful admission, but I couldn't have enjoyed the Depression more. We were poor, but I was never aware of it. The only time I ever cried myself to sleep was when the pangs of what my mother called "growing pains" (it turned out to be incipient rheumatic fever) wracked my legs at night.

What did I know about the economy, about bread-lines and soup kitchens? When we arrived in Vancouver in 1935, I was a rube kid from a tiny little fold in northern B.C.'s brooding immensity and I had been dropped into an adventure of exploration. There was so much to be discovered!

I had never seen cement sidewalks, streetcars, grass lawns, big

buildings, songbirds, beaches, rose bushes, tall street lamps, horses, sailboats, bottled milk, taxicabs, neon lights, elevators, movies, zoo monkeys, ferry boats, soda fountains, buses, gardens or marching bands. Yet here they were and the wonder of them all entranced me. Every day I was eager to burst out the door to find new thrills, oblivious of my mother's warning, "Mind you don't wander too far."

Besides, when you were a child of the thirties, your soul could be bought for a nickel.

You who habitually dump your useless small change, the coppers, nickels and dimes that don't buy anything these days, into a jar, cannot imagine the purchasing power that a five-cent piece, in the grimy fist of a five or six year old, once held. And despite the harsh fact that our family of three subsisted for month after month on the $27.50 per month we received in relief support, augmented by the baked goods my father's sisters pressed on us, I always seemed to be able to wheedle a nickel out of my mother for my discretionary spending.

Five cents bought a half-hour of decision-making in front of the glassed-in penny candy counter at Mac's Confectionery, just down Broadway from our rooming-house. The transaction was showdown time. The sweating, impatient Mac pushing, prodding. ("I got better things to do, y'know.") The kid consumer, heeled with that shiny nickel, not about to be hurried into rash decisions.

What to buy? The chocolate-covered teddy bear? The multicoloured jaw-breakers that lasted for hours? The little hard hats, two for a penny? Nigger bones (sorry, that's what they were called), a licorice pipe, the marshmallow milk bottle with the sweet red stuff inside? The caramel sucker, the hot cinnamon hearts, the goofy wax teeth?

When the selections were made, the goods were packed into a paper bag and the package of riches provided real heft as it was carried off to a secret place, usually behind the advertising billboard in the gully at Broadway and Alder. Friends were seldom invited to share in the several hours of bliss that followed.

All the food essentials cost five cents: chocolate bars, pop, Crackerjacks ("with a prize in each and every box!").

If the nickel was not pumped directly into the belly, there was a variety of five-cent amusement. Take a nickel to the nearest Japanese grocery store and they'd sell you the damnedest kite you ever saw, a gaudy, rice-paper Samurai, made rigid with curved strips of bamboo and wisps of cotton thread, with a paper tail to keep it airborne. You could get a balsa-wood glider and adjust the wing setting to make it do loops and Immelmans. And, hell, if you didn't have a penny in your pocket, you just attached strings to the four corners of a handkerchief, tied the strings to a lead toy soldier and you had a perfect paratrooper. I am both amused and depressed when I hear contemporary kids blame their lawlessness, their ennui, on "boredom." Their problem is not that society is not providing them with recreational facilities. Their problem is that they lack the imagination to provide their own amusement. I cannot remember being bored for a minute of my childhood, not with trees to climb, games of Release to be played, sponge balls to be thrown over roofs, clouds to be examined for hidden faces, bushes to be hidden behind, scooters to be made from wooden crates, store awnings to be jumped at and slapped.

Sometimes the financing got out of hand and required serious saving, nickels and dimes squirrelled away in a sock. The first yo-yos cost a dime. The first bolo bats were two-bits for the cheap, unpainted one, an impossible thirty-five cents for the thick, model, painted red, that whapped the tethered ball with a good, solid sound. And it course, there were maintenance costs: spare yo-yo strings, replacement rubber cords for the bolo bats.

Conversely, when there was just no money at all, Broadway was always a free show. Twice a day the open-topped B.C. Electric observation car went by, with Teddy Lyons and his megaphone describing the route to tourists wrapped in Hudson's Bay blankets. We would wait until it came abreast of us and then bellow, "Rubbernecks" at the passengers, intoxicated at our boldness.

There was so much industrial air pollution from the mills on the

banks of False Creek that when we had fogs, we had genuine London pea-soupers, dirty yellow and foul-smelling, and the streetcars crept through them on Broadway, clanging their bells constantly, their big front lamps looking ghostlike in the swirling murk. But even then, Broadway was beautiful.

For a while, Ronnie and Kenny Bell, my fellow Anyoxers, and I had a good scam going at Broadway and Cambie. There was a bakery there and, one early evening, we were peering through the window, watching the proprietor getting ready to close up. He saw our grubby little faces looking at the cinnamon buns he was removing from the window, beckoned us inside and gave us half a dozen. We went back night after night, getting stale buns. I came home one night, white icing on my face, and my mother dragged the story out of me. We were told, in no uncertain terms, that we might be down but we weren't out enough that we had to beg on the streets.

My mother recalls that a big Saturday night for her and my dad and Jack and Ethel Bell was "walking downtown, looking in the store windows and imagining what we would buy when our ship came in."

Occasionally my parents took me downtown for dinner at the The Old English Fish and Chips, on East Hastings, I believe. A full adult portion of perfect fish and chips, bread and butter and tea, was thirty-five cents. Mine cost twenty-five cents. The place had a gypsy tea-cup reader and a singing cowboy, both of them, I'm sure, depression victims working for tips. I am still mad for fish and chips, still comparing them to the hefty platters at the Old English.

In summer, we took the streetcar to Kitsilano Beach, five cents each way, and got a big cardboard tub of smoking hot, mealy chips for another nickel, with all the malt vinegar we could douse them with. Tied together, the tubs made a fine line of sea-going barges. We were movie-mad and the Saturday matinee at the Stanley Theatre was not to be missed. Once a month my mother would give me a quarter and send me off. I got a ten cent haircut at Granville and Thirteenth (enduring the humiliation of sitting on a plank across the arms of the chair), bought a long-lasting

MacIntosh's Toffee Bar and paid the remaining dime at the box office to see a double feature, the Movietone newsreel, a cartoon and Coming Attractions. When the lights went out, there was a barrage of racket, kids like me banging their MacIntosh's or Pep Chew bars on the wooden arm rests to break them into manageable pieces.

In September I started school, pitched into the white rapids of grade one, equipped only with a precocious ability to read. An upstairs tenant at the Avoca Apartments broke me in on the Oz books, requiring me to give a two-minute oral report on a completed book before lending me the next in the series.

On the first day my mother scrubbed away the accumulated layers of summer grime behind my ears ("you could grow potatoes back there"), dressed me in my best, walked me up Alder Street to Fourteenth and left me at the door of Miss Ingalls's first grade classroom on the main floor of Cecil Rhodes Elementary School.

Ah, Miss Ingalls. My first love. So gorgeous, so good-smelling, so gentle. She actually, in front of the entire class, called me "Little Mr. Big Brown Eyes." On the other hand, she left me marooned at the blackboard one day, despite my frantic requests to leave the room. I stood there and peed my pants. My first evidence that love did not come easily.

At the end on the term, she gave me a gift, a little framed pen and ink drawing of a small boy in a fancy suit, staring up at a chirping song bird in a cage. I still have it. She told my mother, "Dennis is a dreamer, Mrs. Boyd, but don't worry. It's a great gift."

I think she got that part right.

As the 1930s teetered and tottered, limped and lurched towards the uncertain 1940s, my parents and I became convinced we were carrying burdens we would never be allowed to put down.

For my parents, it was the despair of blameless poverty, the seeming impossibility of ever having a few bucks that did not have to be spent right now.

My dad didn't sit around our little basement apartment at 1250

West Broadway wallowing in it. Every morning he went out with a meat paste sandwich in a paper bag and came back home at dinner time. He was just out there, pounding the sidewalks, looking for any kind of day work that might pay a couple of dollars, that might relieve him of all the frustrations of the jobless. But when he came home, all he had been relieved of was the meat paste sandwich. The load was still on his thick shoulders.

Between 1935 and 1940 the only steady work he had was a few months as a mucker at the Britannia Beach mine. The pay was low, the work was hard and dirty and half of his paycheque was sucked up by room and board and boat fare for his weekend trips home.

My burden was Miss Faunt's music classes.

I had left the sweet care of Miss Ingalls in the first grade at Cecil Rhodes Elementary and climbed a couple of branches higher in the education tree, snagging my sweater on a few sharp points.

Miss Faunt was the music teacher for the entire school and my grade four teacher. She was formidable. A short, muscular body, a face as red as a chimney brick. Hair in a tight bun.

I don't know why she scared me but she did. She'd march us to the upstairs music room like little prisoners, arrange us in some order only she understood and command us to sing wonderfully.

Being small, I was always in the front row, so fearful I could only produce hoarse grunts and awful bleats. Some of the worst times of my life were spent watching Miss Faunt's muscular right arm pumping cadence while I tried to stay on the melody, tried to put some feeling, some understanding, into the incomprehensible words "In days of yore, from Britain's shores, Wolfe-the-dauntless-hero-came . . ."

Henry Lyons, being tall, was always in the back row, nicely hidden away. A big redhead, he could stretch his voice up to a remarkable falsetto, miles off key. Miss Faunt could hear it but couldn't place it. It made her furious. We'd have to sing about goddamn Wolfe again and again as Miss Faunt tried to find that phantom falsetto.

Henry Lyons did it, Miss Faunt. It was Henry every time. Will you like me now?

Once, I was in the playground area after school, shooting baskets, showing off for a girl named Barbara. Miss Faunt walked by and stopped. "Shoot it in, Dennis," she said, kindly. I put it up and missed. An air ball. From five feet. Miss Faunt sniffed an it-figures sniff and stalked away, making the earth tremble.

I could have been a somebody in her eyes but I blew the clutch shot. I choked. A couple of days later she gave me a swat alongside the ear for doing something clumsy.

Miss Faunt's favourite was Gerald Jarvis. He was tall and had the soulful eyes of a minor saint and he wore knickers and played the violin. We used to chase him after school and throw his fiddle up in the chestnut trees.

Years later I was listening to a radio fund-raiser for the Vancouver Symphony Orchestra. They said they were proud and honoured to have in the studio the vso's concert master and principal violinist, Gerald Jarvis. I couldn't believe it. I got in my car and drove down to make a pledge and see for myself. It was the same guy from grade school, the same fiddle player. But now he was suave and handsome and he had silver hair, a man of commanding presence. They told me he had an international reputation as a soloist and section leader. No wonder Miss Faunt always liked him best.

When I heard that Miss Faunt had died, quite alone, surrounded by stacks of sheet music and manuscripts, I felt a twinge of remorse that I had never lived up to her expectations if, indeed, she had any expectations at all for me.

At home, I had another presence in my life. My maternal granddad had come to live with us. He had been living in Cedar, south of Nanaimo, but had come to Vancouver to have half of his ulcerated stomach removed. Granddad moved in with us while he recuperated. He arrived at our back door with a big smile, crushing hugs, a rifle, a pound of tripe and a wedge of Gorgonzola cheese that caused houseflies to die in flight when he unwrapped it. He

brought a lot of laughter into our lives, a lot of fascinating stories that he told when he hauled me up on his knee. My mom loved him and so did I. But he was another mouth to feed and, even deprived of half his stomach, Granddad did love to eat.

But just when everything seemed to be at its bleakest, something wonderful happened. The Second War happened. The Depression ended almost overnight and there were jobs for everyone.

I had had vague hints that unusual things were happening, far away and close to home. At school, the Chinese and Japanese kids had become quietly uncomfortable with each other. In the papers, there were pictures of big airplanes and soldiers with bayonets on their rifles. On the radio news, I heard about cities called Chunking and Nanking.

In December my mom gave me a quarter and told me to go down and buy a bag of Christmas oranges. Full of importance I tore down to the Chinese corner grocery store at Broadway and Hemlock and asked for "Two bits worth of Jap oranges." The lady in the store shook her head at me. "No, no," she said. "Jap oranges bad. You buy Mandarin oranges."

On another day I was out on the vacant lot next to the White Rose Ballroom, playing with a nickel glider. Suddenly I heard newsboys running up both sides of Broadway, bellowing. They were yelling "Extra, extra!" (they actually used to say that, just like in the movies) and barking out words about a Blitz, about Bombers over London.

I went inside and asked my mom about it. She told me that people, countries, sometimes fought with each other. She said that when she was a little girl in England, she saw the German zeppelins. But she said that everything would be all right in the end. And she put on the whistling tea kettle to make a pot of tea.

Not long afterward my Granddad left us. He gave me some more of his bone-crushing hugs and said that he would be seeing me soon. The next thing I knew we were packing and moving to Victoria.

Chapter 3

Granddad's first attempt at family reunification was not a great bellowing success.

With the outbreak of the Second World War in September 1939, the Depression ended abruptly and the comatose Canadian economy rejigged itself for war production. Suddenly there were jobs, good paying ones, for the asking. For Granddad, it was a second call to arms and, for an old man, he responded briskly.

He moved to Victoria and almost immediately got a job as foreman-of-the-ways, responsible for keel-layings and launchings of the ten-thousand-ton freighters and the marvellous Royal Canadian Navy corvettes contracted to the Victoria Machinery Depot on Bay Street. Granddad immediately wrote to us, saying that he had a job for my dad and a rented house we could all live in.

Well, the job was legitimate. My dad become a shipwright at more money per hour than he had ever dreamed of. But the house was a bummer. It was down at the foot of Tattersal Drive in Victoria's Cloverdale district. It was big and it was solid. But it had only two doors, front and back, and none inside. The third door was on the outhouse, fifty feet down a bramble-covered dirt path on a soggy back yard that never drained or dried out.

My mother was appalled. She let Granddad know that she hadn't survived the Depression to settle for outdoor plumbing and no indoor privacy. Granddad found another place for us, a little bungalow out on Carey Road in South Saanich, three miles from

downtown Victoria. The rooms were small — the largest was the attached garage where we stored cord wood and sawdust — but it had a big back yard and an unfinished attic that was eventually converted into my bedroom. Until it was built, I slept on a cot in the kitchen, being awakened every time the sawdust hopper gulped and blew back.

The exterior of the house was covered with what was called broken-bottle stucco, and it was just that. Chunks of multicoloured broken bottle-glass were applied to the drying matrix. It was considered attractive, but it was a bitch when I was first learning to ride a bicycle, wobbled around the side of the house and put out a hand to steady myself. I had lacerated palms for a year.

Eventually my Auntie Mae came to live with us and to work at the VMD and we took in a boarder, Tony, a VMD carpenter. It was crowded but it was lively.

It seemed close to town but we were in the sticks. We had a tin mailbox out front, right on an open ditch. Our telephone, the first we'd ever had, had a crank handle on the right side to call Central. Our party line number was Colquitz 67X, and when we heard two short rings and a long, it was for us.

Here, in this little bungalow, we had the happiest times of our life as a family. Granddad played lord of the manor and my mom let him get away with it, though she handled the budget and made the important decisions.

Everybody loved my grandfather. Some of my friends asked if they could call him Granddad. His own friends called him Uncle Bill.

William Hillary Sager was born in England during the Victorian era. He married young and fathered four children, sons Reg and Ernie, daughters Irene and Mae. Trained in shipyards, he joined the Royal Navy at the outbreak of the First World War and served in the Mediterranean, in Gibraltar, Malta and around Turkey. He used to tell me hair-raising stories about Lascars and Goanese and Turkish soldiers who sold the dried, severed ears of their battle victims as souvenirs. I still have a fez that he brought home from the

war. My Aunt Mae had a necklace made from a flint arrowhead Granddad found on Crete. Any time I was finicky at the dinner table, he'd tell me how lucky I was to have such wonderful food as parsnips. He said that "When we were in Gib, we lived for days on soup made of grass, mice and whiskey." He also gave me my first cooking lesson, as defined by the RN cooks: "When it's brown it's baked; when it's black it's buggered."

Granddad suffered the serviceman's second greatest fear next to a physical wound. He got a Dear Bill letter. While he was serving, his wife, the grandmother I know nothing of, ran away with another man, leaving the four children temporarily orphaned. Granddad had to come home on compassionate leave to find homes for his brood. He did it. He found foster homes for all of them. My mother recalls being in a private school for a while, "at tuppence per week."

Eventually Granddad brought his motherless kids to Canada and, blessed with a good solid work ethic, they found their own homes.

In the house on Carey Road, he was with his two daughters, and Ernie and his family lived a mile down the road. Reg, the eldest, was in Port Hardy.

Granddad was a great influence in my growing up, moreso than my own father. I don't think my dad ever had a real boyhood. Life was hard and mean in Govan and he was doing a man's work in the Clyde River shipyards when he was fourteen. He had a good sense of humour but not much sense of play. We never had a game of catch, never went fishing together. But he worked his behind off and he was good to my mother.

Granddad was different. Part of him had never grown up. He would give me a rap on the ear if he heard me sassing my parents, but he would also sneak up on me, thrown me on the floor and tickle me until I was breathless with laughter. I would take other kids home with me to watch Granddad put his thumb in his mouth, blow and inflate his bicep. He played his first game of golf when he was in his sixties, a VMD tournament, had the highest

score in the tournament but came home roaring about the bunker shot he holed on the sixteenth hole. He won a set of clubs, which he gave to me, a few of which I passed on to my son.

The first time I ever went saltwater fishing, Granddad and I took a rod and a bag of sandwiches on a bus and a streetcar to the Ogden Point breakwater. I cast out a line baited with pileworms and immediately got snagged on the bottom. Granddad warned me not to fall in and said he'd be back and took off. Half an hour later I saw a rowboat coming around a corner. There was Granddad, his back straight and stiff, the muscles in his arms rippling in the sun. He helped me into the rowboat, said he had "found it" and told me to haul in my fish. I reeled in and be damned, just as he said, there was a fat red snapper on it. Later, I caught a hefty rock cod. We hauled the catch home and had it for supper. The next day, we all came down with diarrhea. Never fish near an industrial outflow.

Granddad loved his food. He especially loved great thick Sunday roasts of beef, the fat untrimmed. He would caution my mom, "Irene, don't throw away the dripping, it's the best part." The rest of the week he would snack on the white, congealed beef fat slathered on bread. He claimed to be deaf in one ear, which justified the hearty, happy way he slurped soup. My mother tried to modify his bachelor table manners, but it was no use. Once, we had guests, a couple of lonely Royal Air Force airmen from the Patricia Bay air base, for Sunday dinner. Midway, Granddad put down his busy knife and fork and picked up a bottle of Garton's savoury meat sauce. After studying the label he announced, "You know, if you spell Garton's backwards it's Snotrag."

Every time the VMD launched a freighter or corvette, Granddad wore a suit and tie to work because he was the man in charge. He made sure there were tons of chains attached to the bow, to provide drag when the vessel hit the water. He made sure the ways were thoroughly greased and that the chocks were knocked out with huge mauls in the proper order to release the hull. When the ship was free and floating and whistles were blowing around the harbour, Granddad proudly shook hands with every man on his

crew. Bottles, forbidden, were opened and quickly passed around, and another keel was laid.

At one point, Granddad, my dad, Uncle Ernie, Auntie Mae, Tony the boarder and my cousin Jack Patterson, who was the amateur heavyweight boxing champion of Canada, all worked at the VMD. Cousin Jack set a Canadian shipyards record for the number of rivets driven in a single day.

But the war ended and so did the jobs, as Canada quickly geared down from wartime production. My dad, who had tried several times to join the wartime Navy but was prevented by the Essential Services Act, got house-building work. Granddad kept building boats, little ones. He rented a big old barn and began building exquisite ten-foot clinker-built rowboats. I got to help him steam the hull-planks in a long, narrow box over a steam heater until they were as pliable as cooked linguine. I also got to hold the bronze bucking-up rod, inside the upside down hull, as he clinched the copper roves into the copper nails, making a perfect water-tight seal.

Later he moved to Saltspring Island, to a little waterfront shack at Ganges, where he supplemented his pension money by building Tonkin split-cane flyrods. When I asked him where he learned to build rowboats and fishing rods, he gave me a little cuff on the arm and said, "Sailors learn to do anything that involves water, except to drown in it."

He shared his cabin and his life with a little owl that he found injured, nursed to health and called Joey. He was determined to teach Joey to speak. I think Joey thought Granddad was his mother because he nested and slept in Granddad's clothes. One day Granddad came in from a beach walk, sank into his favourite chair and crushed Joe to death, hidden in a shirt. Granddad was heartbroken. Joey was the first of his children he saw die.

Granddad was over seventy when his life of adventure ended. I miss him. But if he was still around, he'd be about 120 years old and a bit too stiff for pulling me down and tickling me. And I finally figured out that blowing-up-the-bicep trick.

I think I was ten or eleven years old the first time it happened, the dark thing.

I can't think of any reason why it happened when it did. Maybe it was there all the time, waiting to happen, a damaged gene, flickering erratically.

We were in Victoria then and life was really terrific. The ship-yards in Victoria were booming. We had plenty of money. I got two-bits allowance a week whether I earned it or not. The house was warm and we had roast beef for dinner every Sunday.

I hadn't felt any wrench at all in leaving Vancouver. I couldn't know it but in 1942, all the Japanese kids I had gone to school with at Cecil Rhodes, including my buddy Yuki, who lived down at Sixth and Alder, had vanished almost overnight, taken away with their families to internment camps in remote parts of the interior to get them away from the coast. Paranoia, racism and greed were running a three-legged race in the early forties.

I didn't think much of Victoria's streetlights. Most of them had flower pots on the tops, with geraniums and petunias trailing down the poles. But I was pretty happy in Victoria. I had made a set of new friends quickly, I was enjoying school, I enjoyed the safe excitement of being a young spectator to the war. Quite often Bren-gun carriers rattled past our street, leaving tread-grooves in the asphalt. Even as far out as we were, we could hear the whoop-whoop-whoop sound of destroyers and corvettes entering and leaving the harbour. We would see training planes from Pat Bay airport flying over the harbour, trailing drogue targets on long cables, and brown smudges of anti-aircraft fire all around them. We'd sit in vacant fields and cheer the hits.

All the kids learned to recognize the silhouettes of British, American, German and Japanese fighters and bombers. We all figured we'd be the first to turn in the alarm when the first Mitsubishi bomber flew over Victoria. My dad and three other neighbourhood men were the Air-Raid Precaution team and I was their messenger, me with my green bike with the loose seat that flopped up when I pedalled standing up, causing me to sit down

on bare bolts. The ARP team had a bucket of sand, a bucket of water and a foot-operated stirrup pump. With this they were supposed to douse the magnesium incendiary bombs that were expected. We had one night drill, figured out the odds against us and pretty much turned the firefighting responsibilities over to the care of God, or Churchill or whoever.

I was doing pretty well in school and going to Sunday school under protest. Our Sunday school teacher was a spooky guy who used to stop us on the street or on the bus during the week, warning us that we would fry in hell if we didn't get down on our knees and pray for forgiveness. I even sang in the church choir. The lady who directed us lived on a big farm and often smelled of cows. But she was easier to take than that Sunday school teacher. Rather than put Jesus into my heart, he scared Him right out of me.

We went to the war movies and cheered Churchill, Roosevelt and Stalin equally in the newsreels and figured Mackenzie King looked like a bit of dope compared to the other leaders. We would trade anything we owned for a white American sailor hat. We removed the pins from Canadian Army Artillery cap badges and hammered them into rings that turned our fingers green. At school we did marching drill with broomsticks for rifles and we collected aluminum and tinfoil and old tires and filled our dad's tobacco tins with leftover fat and bought war savings stamps at two-bits a week, which was a 100 per cent drain on my pocket money. It was all for the war effort, we were told. One day we were cleaning out a little shed behind the school where we stored all the salvageable materials we had collected. We were using a bucket brigade. I turned my head at the wrong time (I had very little sense of rhythm), a loaded bucket hit my elbow and dislocated it. It looked awful but didn't hurt much. The girls squealed. Mr. MacDonald, our grade six teacher, grabbed my arm and snapped it back into place. I was a hero for days, me and my war wound.

There were always big doings at our place on Saturday nights. We seemed to be Party Central for the shipyard workers, all the Anyox expatriates and anyone from Scotland. Liquor rationing was

a bit of a problem but one that was usually solved. One bottle of overproof Navy-issue rum, about twice the potency of the rationed stuff in the liquor stores, could keep a party going to midnight. And everyone knew a sailor or a bootlegger.

I enjoyed those parties, what I saw of them. My mom used to make baking powder biscuits and pop them in the oven with grated cheese on top. I gorged on them. By the time I was upstairs in bed, they'd be into the sing-song. "I Belong to Glasgow," popular Hit Parade songs, Gracie Fields songs, the "North Atlantic Squadron." There was one something about "Roll Me Over in the Clover." I thought it was some kind of counting song they must have learned when they were in school.

One night, when I was up later than usual, my mom asked me to take a tray of glasses into the kitchen. I noticed that one of the glasses still had about an inch or so of stuff in it, with a wedge of lemon. My dad was famous for his hot rums, dark rum, brown sugar, lemon, boiling water. I was curious, so I bolted it down, alone in the kitchen.

If it had been whiskey, I probably would have thrown it right back up. But I felt this drink go right down to my feet, back up and take a warm, muzzy feeling into my brain. I thought I understood why everyone at our parties was so happy. It was the brown stuff in the glasses. It tasted good and felt good. I really didn't give it a second thought. Later in my life, I wouldn't be able to think about anything else.

Can you have an epiphany when you are ten or eleven years old?

I can't figure out which were the most wasted four years of my life, my high school years or 1970 to 1973, when I was pretty much shit-faced and out of it. During the drinking period, I did have the odd moment of complete clarity. I had damned few of them in high school. I was too busy memorizing useless trivia.

I came into high school ready to learn, ready to grow up, ready to chase babes. In the last years of elementary school, we heard that all the girls in high school would have boobs and would know

everything about, you know, doing it. What a load of disappointment we ran into. I went into high school a virgin, came out a virgin and my mind didn't expand any more than my body did.

I believe successful education involves the process of making the young person teachable. That involves making the student eager to learn and able to learn. For that to happen, learning habits have to be developed before the first textbook is cracked, before the first Friday snap quiz is held.

Nobody ever taught me how to take notes, how to condense notes, how to organize study time, how to research, how to prepare effectively for examinations.

I had no idea how to learn on my own so I followed the teacher's lead. I held still while they opened up a lid on top of my head and poured in bucket after bucket of things-you'd-better-remember. For four years they poured this crap into my head. Dates of famous revolutions. Geometric theorems. French idioms. Bits of poetry. Famous seaports. Neat things Napoleon may or may not have said. Stuff you should never mix in the same laboratory beaker. Nobody ever told me why it was important to memorize, beyond using it to navigate past the deadly shoals of the midterm exam. I don't think I was dumb in high school but I sure as hell graded out dumb.

I was playing football all this time. I was a quarterback. When our coach gave me a list of plays I might call on second down and four, he patiently told me the function of each play and why it might work on a wet field but not a dry field, why it would be a good call on their ten-yard line but disastrous on our ten. Not only was I learning what to do, but I knew why I should do it. I enjoyed that thinking process. I was proud to be put in charge of it.

No teacher ever gave me that much slack, that much credit. So I crawled through the first three years and almost fell apart in my senior year. I had to get outside tutoring in my last year of French, or my teacher, the stern but fair Miss Piggott, assured me, I would flunk the year. That meant I wouldn't make university entrance requirements. My parents wisely told me they weren't about to pay

for my tutoring; it was my fault for screwing up, my problem to overcome. Fortunately I had a part-time job, delivering telegrams for the CPR, that supplied the cash for my French cramming. I passed the French final and qualified to take two years at Victoria College. That charming school, with its tiny, exquisite campus and its superb faculty, was everything that my high school wasn't. I did quite well in the courses I wanted and found out that I had a reasonably high IQ, not genius by any means, but not sea-level, as I had believed in those four demoralizing high school years.

As it turned out, I didn't need high school, except as a boot camp towards college. To borrow and break another quote, everything I needed to know I learned in grade seven. Robert Fulghum, a philosopher-preacher from Seattle, got himself rich and on the top of the New York *Times* best-seller list with a little book called *All I Ever Needed to Know I learned in Kindergarten*. Over a sushi lunch in Vancouver in 1989, I told the charming Fulghum that it had taken until grade seven for me to make my learning breakthrough. "Slow learner," he said, as he scissored up a piece of raw mackerel with his chopsticks.

I guess all of us has a character in our lives who we never forget, who burns some kind of brand in us that never wears off. Mine was the man who gave me my career.

I did two things in grade seven. I threw up on Eddie Burkmar and I learned to write proper sentences.

Throwing up on poor Eddie was my mom's fault. I came home for lunch every day from MacKenzie Avenue School. It was a block away and mom insisted I have a hot lunch. I was a finicky eater, used to drive my Granddad crazy. "Let your meat stop your mouth," he'd growl when I started whining about what was on my plate.

What was on my plate for lunch this day was a bowl of Campbell's bean soup. I didn't like it. Mom said I'd sit there until I finished it. Afraid of being late, I got it down and ran like hell back to school. Five minutes into the first afternoon class, up it came and out it went, all over Eddie Burkmar, a harmless guy who sat in

front of me. He made a sound like a trombone. I fled to the boys' room in the basement. The humiliation was dreadful, but it was a normal enough thing to happen in a roomful of forty young kids. Why do I remember it with such clarity?

Well, never mind that. The important thing that happened to me in grade seven was a man named Mr. Garner — W. G. Garner. Pop, we called him. He was a dumpy little Irishman, mostly bald, with a Churchillian face and just a residual wisp of white hair. At one time he had led safaris in Africa and he often spoke to us in Swahili. When he said, "Bureeka," it meant move and we moved. He told anyone he spotted as a potential trouble-maker, "You and I are going to fight and you're a fool because I'll win." He called me Dinny.

He came to our little elementary school, as principal and grade seven and eight teacher, in the last year of his career. The previous year he had been principal at Mount View High School, where I was to spend those four crummy years.

He was a shrewd judge of character, particularly when it came to dealing with tough kids. After the Christmas holidays, a brother and sister came into our class, new arrivals from the Interior. The girl, Annie, was tough enough, but the brother, Jimmy, was a terror. Out on the school grounds, he discouraged any hasty friendships by winning a series of one-punch fights. In class, he simply refused to speak. On top of that, he wore the empty holster from a cap gun set. It flapped when he walked and fascinated us.

It took Pop Garner a month to figure Jimmy out. He tried his famous "You and I are going to fight . . ." ultimatum early on and got, after the "I'll win" punchline, a long silence, followed by a grim "Maybe not." This was unbelievable. This was mutiny.

Mr. Garner bided his time. He moved Jimmy to the front of a row. He began to ask Jimmy to run errands, to pass our papers, to see that the class kept quiet while he was out of the room. He made Jimmy his aide-de-camp. Jimmy loved it. To the most casual request he would leap to his feet, slamming his boots down like a recruit on a drill square and stand at attention, quivering. He'd answer, "Yes *sirrrr*"

Jimmy stopped wearing the gun holster. He quit punching the snot out of the rest of us. He got good marks. By the end of the year I think he and Mr. Garner loved each other. I don't know what kind of background Jimmy came from, but I suspect Mr. Garner was the first adult to treat him with respect.

Mr. Garner came to our school as a maverick within the school district. He still gave the strap. (I got two whacks across the ass from him for a silly April Fool's Day prank.) He once sent me out to pinch some pears for him from a nearby tree. And he ignored the approved school curriculum and taught us as he saw fit, God bless his Irish soul. He taught us to parse sentences, just as he had learned to parse Latin in his own school years.

In terms of learning to speak and write coherently, correctly, parsing is simplicity and perfection. It had been dropped from the high school curriculum years before Mr. Garner came to our school, abandoned as being too cumbersome, too archaic, perhaps too British old-school even for Victoria. Yet Pop Garner taught it to us in grade seven.

I'm damned if I know how anyone can learn sentence structure without it. Parsing is simply an analytical breakdown of sentences. Each word is given an identity and a function. The relationship between the words is established. You identify the subject, predicate and object of each sentence. You connect the nouns with the pronouns, connect the verbs with the adverbs, shove the prepositions in the right place and, before you know it, you have built a sentence that will pass the quality examination at the end of the word-assembly line. Put a few of those correct sentences together, you have a paragraph. It's just like building a car — you better not start before you have been through the parts department a few times. Yet teachers I speak to tell me they have never heard of parsing or that it sounds dreadfully complicated or that it smacks of fascism.

Admittedly, it baffled me in grade seven. Then, on one golden, glorious day, it all came to me, in a rush. Suddenly, I understood. I could take apart a sentence and put it back together without dangling a modifier. At that moment, I knew that I knew how to write

and I was right: I did know. It didn't help me in high school, where all they wanted was one-word recitations, regurgitated like that still-warm bean soup I horked over Eddy Burkmar. But that ability to put thoughts on paper, logically and clearly, was a priceless gift in college, where a three-hour exam might consist of four questions, beginning with the words, "Discuss in five hundred words . . ." I could ace that kind of question, even with minimal knowledge of the subject, because I could use the five hundred words effectively, if not entirely knowledgeably.

I loved every day of my two years in college. In an early philosophy class the delightful Dr. Ewing, a brilliant, twinkly educator, discussed a few of Hegel's thoughts at some length and then turned to me and asked, " And what do you think of that, Mr. Boyd?" I was stunned. A teacher was asking me what I thought, instead of warning me to memorize it before Christmas. I felt like I was out of jail and the warden was offering me his car.

Determined to cram as much practical knowledge as I could into two years — I had an inkling that I wanted to write for a living — I set up my own liberal arts program. I took philosophy, psychology, sociology and all the English they would allow me. I did quite well in everything I wanted and needed. I was an utter, flunking disaster in the courses I didn't want but was required to take: maths, French and geography. In second year, the registrar told me no one could take English 200 and 205 in the same year. Too many papers to write. I insisted on taking the chance. So did one other guy. We both passed both courses handsomely and have both profited immensely from the experience and the knowledge gained from taking three years of English in two years. The other guy who shared the pain of all those papers was Gerry, who was a dead look-alike for Charles Laughton, and who once shared a silver flask of gin with me before an English final. He is currently known as Mr. Justice Gerald R. B. Coultas of the Supreme Court of British Columbia.

Without the leg up on English I got in grade seven, I might not have survived high school; I might have quit to follow an appren-

ticeship in upholstering that I had begun during summer holidays. I might never have gone to college and discovered I'm not a dunce. I might never have gone into journalism and I surely would not be writing this book.

Thank you, Mr. Garner. Thank you for everything I have.

Chapter 4

I can remember almost every word of the first story I got published in a newspaper. I'm still a bit embarrassed about it. I wasn't answering the call of journalism, I just wanted to get my name in the paper. Maybe that's what still drives me.

I was about sixteen, in high school and playing football for the James Bay Athletic Association, a sports club that had a hundred-year history in rowing and rugby. We won a game 6-0 and I scored the only touchdown on a five-yard quarterback sneak. Okay, okay, it was two yards. That night I scribbled out a three-paragraph report on the game. I reported that Dennis Boyd scored the only touchdown on a six-yard quarterback sneak. I phoned the sports department of the *Victoria Colonist*. The assistant sports editor, a nice guy (I later discovered) named Jim Eddy, took the score and was agreeably pleased when I said I had the game story. I dictated it, he thanked me, told me to keep him up to date on our league, and the story, my story, was there in print the next morning, word for self-aggrandizing word.

By the damnedest coincidence, one of my classmates, who reported high school sports for the *Colonist*, and who knew I was interested in a journalism career, told me he was tired of working for lousy space rates and was quitting. I called Jim Eddy, identified myself as his junior football correspondent, and got the vacant job. Not only that, I started getting general sports assignments that paid about twelve cents a column inch. I had my foot in.

I got in up to my knee while attending a senior softball game at

Central Park. Someone said to me, "See that guy sitting out in deep left field? That's Pete Sallaway, the *Victoria Times* sports editor. Nobody else but Pete could get away with sitting out there, but nobody messes with him." I said, "I'm going out there to talk to him." My friend said, "Jeez, don't do that. Don't bother him. He hasn't got any upper teeth but he'll still bite your ass off."

I walked out there. He was sitting under a huge chestnut tree, a few feet behind the left fielder. I noticed two things about him. He had a great dog, a Chesapeake retriever. He was wearing the most terrific pair of gleaming cordovan loafers I had ever seen. ("These guys must earn a fortune", I thought.) And, clearly, he did not have any upper teeth. I introduced myself, told him I wanted to be a sportswriter and waited for him to tell me to bugger off. He couldn't have been more gracious. Told me to sit down, asked me about my schooling and said, "If you make it, you won't make any money, but you'll have more fun that you have a right to have."

I got just one assignment from Pete, but it required me to go into the old *Times* newsroom on Fort Street to write my story instead of phoning it in. I went in at night. The sports department was deserted, but there were a few reporters in the newsroom. The smell of the place, the thick, musty, intoxicating smell of it! Cigars and pipe smoke, library paste, sweat, brilliantine and possibly cheap whiskey. I rolled a piece of paper into any upright typewriter and started sweating my lead. One of the reporters, in a white shirt, tie and vest, came over and asked me what I was doing. I told him I was a sports stringer.

"Going to get into the business?" he asked.

"Hope so," I said.

"Well, look, kid, in the business, you have to make two dupes of your story. You take three pieces of copy paper, two pieces of carbon paper and make a sandwich. One graph on the first take and don't forget to slug your name over your lead. Close it off with 30."

The jargon enraptured me. The next couple of days, I must have been a pain in the patoot to my friends at school, rambling away about dupes and slugs. But I was learning a lesson: Rather than

41

being the egotistical, cold-blooded sons-of-bitches they seemed to be in the movies, newspaper guys were kind and encouraging to anyone they let come even a short distance into their world.

I finished high school (hated it), I finished college (loved every precious minute), but, other than the rare feat of doing three years of English in two, I didn't have much that was marketable. Some of my Friday night beer-drinking buddies had decided to be teachers and they were going to Normal School. I didn't have any plans or prospects so I decided to go along. Maybe I could teach English. It was a horrible mistake and I bailed out after one week. I got a job with the civil service, as a junior clerk in the Land Registry Office. Hated that, too. Wrestling those huge ledgers, recording Deeds and Conveyances with a wooden pen, I felt that I was in a Dickensian time warp.

While this was happening, the *Victoria Times* promoted Pete Sallaway to telegraph editor and brought in Bill Walker, just out of the Royal Canadian Air Force, as the new sports editor. Nicknamed Sonny, Walker, a terrific baseball and basketball player before the war, had piloted light bombers in North Africa, surviving a couple of crashes. Walker completely revolutionized sportswriting in Victoria. Previously, both papers had filled their sports pages with wire copy, dull, safe writing and syndicated American columnists. Walker brought in a cheeky, personal style of writing to his pages and to his column. God, how I wanted to be on those pages. But all I got was the occasional basketball and lacrosse assignment, at those lousy space rates.

I was numbly entering Sales Conveyances one day when I was called to a telephone. (My job was so low level I didn't rate one.) It was Walker. "Terry's leaving to join the RCMP. His job's available if you want it." I didn't tell him I'd get back to him. Choirs of angels sang from on high.

Walker told me there was one last hurdle: "Archie has to okay you."

That was Archie Wills, the managing editor, a tremendously respected and talented editor, writer and historian. In the last year

of his distinguished career, he had a bit of a cracker-barrel look about him, given to armbands on his shirt and long, thoughtful pauses while he sucked his teeth. "Sonny says he thinks you can handle the job. What do you think?"

I mumbled something.

"Okay, you're hired. The starting pay is thirty-five bucks a week."

I didn't jump up in the air.

"Anything wrong with that?" he asked.

"Well," I said "I have two years of college and I can write."

Wills hooked his thumbs under his suspenders and sucked his teeth. Christ, I thought, I've blown it.

"Two years of college, is it," he said said with exaggerated politeness. "In that case, I guess I'll have to give you $37.50. But you'd better be good."

I was grinning like a carp when I told Walker that Wills had hired me and that I can beaten him on salary. He let out one grunt of laughter. " I guess he gave you that $35 bullshit. The starting guild minimum is $37.50."

Welcome to the newspaper business, kid.

In terms of learning my lifetime craft, I couldn't have landed at a better paper at a better time. Stu Keate, fresh from *Time Magazine*, was the new publisher. He was to become my tolerant, pushing patron. The editor was Bruce Hutchison, the greatest journalist in Canadian history. When Wills retired, during my first six months, the energetic Les Fox, a man who wrote so fast he destroyed typewriters, came in from the *Vancouver Sun's* legislative bureau to run the newsroom. Lloyd Baker, another RCAF vet, was the city editor, getting maximum reporting mileage out of a fascinating collection of news reporters. Every morning, as each reporter came in from his beat, Baker would demand, "Have you got a new?"

I was third man in the sports department. The assistant sports editor was a guy named Lance Whittacker. He was from Anyox. Go figure.

Walker was a hard driver, demanding, seldom given to praise, but he was a good teacher. Had a quirky sense of humour. He sent

me out one day to act as coxswain on the JBAA eight-oared rowing crew. He said it would make a good feature and I could write it in first person.

Christ it was cold. Bundled up, I sat in the stern of that little shell and counted strokes as we knifed down the Gorge and out through the water to the breakwater and back again. When we got back to the crew's clubhouse and the crew members hauled me gingerly out before I put my foot through the hull, I noticed Bill Halkett, one of our photographers, waiting for us, bundled up against the freezing wind in an overcoat. I grumped to him, with my third-man authority, "We've finished. You missed the whole thing." Not quite. The guys picked me up and tossed me into that icy water in the traditional coxswain's dunk, according to Walker's suggestion. Halkett's picture caught me upside down in midair. But it did make a good feature.

We worked hard and we learned to work fast. We were in at 7 A.M. and had to have our three pages of edited copy downstairs in the composing room by 9:30 A.M.

The first time Walker left me in charge of the pages while he was on a road trip, I almost hyperventilated fighting that deadline. But I made it. I supervised the page lock-up, corrected the page proofs and was taking my first deep breath when Alex Donaldson, the printer who made up our pages, came flying through the newsroom, waving a page proof, a look of white death on his face. "The goddamn pages are locked up and on their way. Please tell me you caught this on the fly." I looked where his inky finger was pointed. It was an agate scoreline over a hockey summary and as God was my disbelieving witness, it said, in tiny 6½ point type that got bigger by the second, "Vancouver 3, Victoria Piss All." My heart stopped. I heard it go clunk and stop beating. I was about to faint, perhaps to die, when Alex started to shiver with laughter. It was all a put-up, a traditional composing room test of the new guy's nerves and sense of humour.

We all drank at that paper, from the bosses down to the office boys. We drank good stuff when it was free, cheap stuff when we

were buying it. Another morning, I came up from the composing room wheezing and sniffing with a cold. John Shaw, ex-Royal Canadian Navy and the assistant city editor, whispered that I looked like crap and that he had a bottle, a whole quart, of Walker's Special Rye, the $3.65 stuff, hidden in the janitor's closet down the hall. I walked nonchalantly down there, opened the door, pulled down the familiar brown bottle with the vertical ribbing and took a monster snort. It hit bottom and half of it bounced up and bubbled out of my nose. Shaw's bottle was behind a bucket. I had grabbed the bottle in which the janitor kept his liquid green soap.

Another incident wasn't nearly so funny. Walker was out of town again, I was in charge. I spent the night in the wardroom of a Canadian cruiser, the guest of an officer who had been a college classmate. The drinks were fifteen cents each and my civilian money was no good. I got monstrously drunk. I got home by cab, but I was too far gone to hear the alarm ring in the morning. I missed my whole work shift. I came to at lunch time with a spittingly angry Pete Sallaway shaking me. He told me that they had phoned and phoned and that he had to put out my pages, the paper had been late and that Fox was waiting for me. Sick with hangover and shame, I went in and told Fox the truth. In those days, drunkenness was a reasonable excuse for screwing up. I should have learned some sort of a message from the disgraceful bollix. I should have seen that I tended to forget everything else when the booze was flowing. But I didn't. I was a newspaperman. I was having fun.

I had to be up at 6 A.M., grab a breakfast I could carry and walk half a mile to catch the first bus to town to be in on time for my 7 A.M. shift in the sports department.

We worked five-and-a-half days a week, and one of us came in for a couple of hours on Sunday to sort through the wire copy and rewrite the local sports stories from the Sunday *Colonist*. Overtime pay for night assignments was out of the question. So were expenses.

I recall waiting for a bus to take me to the airport for an assignment in Vancouver — my first airplane trip. In the depot I ordered the baked beans on toast, an irresistible bargain at thirty-five cents and wondered if I should put it on my expense account. Here I was, not out of town yet, and spending company money like a madman. I never once took a cab on company business; the buses and street-cars went everywhere and I had strong young legs for walking.

There were compensations. We got a free turkey for Christmas. On rare occasions there might be a five dollar bonus for outstanding work. It was understood that the windfall money would be used to buy a bottle that would be shared by all comers in the darkroom.

Newsroom boss Les Fox was always on a tight budget and he could squeeze a dollar until the monarch moaned.

We put out a good paper, a damned good bright, lively, occasionally cheeky, liberal-leaning paper. But we never caught the conservative *Colonist* which, drab as it was, had a solid up-Island circulation base that kept us in second place.

In short, it was heaven.

The years I spent at the *Times*, 1951 to 1957, were a marvellous learning experience and, in some ways, a continuing party — bottles hidden in desk drawers and wastepaper baskets, reporters getting polluted enough to tell the bosses off — much like the police press room in the play *The Front Page*.

Bill Walker taught me sternly but he taught me well. He wanted bright writing and he wanted it right bloody now. We worked at a fever pitch and regularly blew out typewriters. And he was generous in sharing the road trips. I went to Peterborough for a Mann Cup Canadian lacrosse championship. I followed our Class B baseball team on a two-week bus trip through Vancouver, Seattle, Spokane, Yakima and Wenatchee. It was on that trip that I had my first exposure to American racism. The lesson came from a middle-aged sports editor in the Spokane press box. Laughing himself breathless when a black Victoria player was knocked down by a high, inside pitch, the guy hollered, "Pitch him tighter. You can't

hurt a nigger hitting him on the head." He had his young son in the press box with him, presumably to follow in daddy's footsteps.

I also learned that minor league ballplayers, making maybe $125 a month, got $5 a day in meal money, and that the married guys saved half of it to send home by simply starving themselves. One guy, a talented shortstop, used to limit himself to candy bar and a bottle of Squirt, twenty cents total, at lunch.

The trainer on that ball club was a guy named Jack Bogue. The players called him Stink. I thought it was horribly cruel until he called me one morning and said, "This is Stink. Bus leaves in twenty minutes."

I travelled by train from Victoria to Brandon, hitting all the prairie cities in the Western Hockey League, with the Victoria Cougars. Early in the trip a very good defenceman, a Boston Bruins farmhand, got whacko in a Calgary beer parlour and fell off a table, where he had been demonstrating Ukrainian dancing. He broke his ankle badly. His teammates carried him back to the hotel and the team trainer, sworn to secrecy, fed him painkillers all night. They carried him to the rink for morning workout, he managed to pull on his skates without screaming, got on the ice and fell down at the very first opportunity, officially breaking his ankle in the line of duty. The ruse saved his paycheque but not his career.

I was pretty naive in those days, deadly serious about my job and I watched my drinking carefully. I watched the professional athletes quietly, from a distance. They weren't all that whackier than some of the amateurs I had played with. Walker told me, "Don't make friends with them. You'll have to turn on them some day." So we drank with the managers but never the players, and eventually we had to turn on the managers.

Our police reporter, Roy Thorsen, who had fought his way through the Sicily and Italian campaigns with the Canadian infantry, contributed two fish and game columns a week for a few extra bucks, but eventually Fox and Walker decided that I could do it for nothing. I didn't particularly like it, but it was my first crack at column

writing. I even took up fishing to provide some authenticity but I never caught anything worth writing about. Eventually, Keate figured I was ready for prime time and gave me a Saturday column on the second sports page. Had my picture on it and everything. About all I can say is that I never got the paper sued. And I was kept humble when Joe Eastick, the assistant composing room foreman, would come upstairs and ask me, "Got that Saturday shit ready yet?"

I was never aware that Keate was keeping a paternal eye on me, but he was. When he dreamed up the circulation stunt of the half-century, the challenge to swim from Victoria to Port Angeles, he detached me from sports to write daily reports and to ghost daily front page columns for distance swimmers Florence Chadwick and Marilyn Bell. The build-up for the Chadwick swim became an international story for weeks and I was right in the middle. But it fizzled. Chadwick hit that icy water off Beacon Hill Park, it brought on her menstrual period prematurely and she barely swam out of sight. That was it for her, but the challengers came by the dozens. Bell made it on her second try, a logger named Ben Laughren did it, but the best swim of all was made by Canada's Cliff Lumsden who, like Bell, was a protégé of Gus Ryder, the great Canadian swimming coach. Only a few of us accompanied him on a small tugboat — the story was getting old — and we were ready to haul him in when his legs cramped up after a few miles. But he kept swimming with his arms, dragging his legs. He swam through the sunset, swam through the night, swam through the rips and jellyfish until, through the darkness, we saw the light on Ediz Hook, east of Port Angeles. I took a rowboat and a lantern, jumped into the surf and set the lantern on a rock. He came pounding into the light, throwing up a roostertail of spray with his shoulders. It was the damnedest feat of raw strength and brute determination I have ever seen.

I went back to the sports department after the first wave of swimmers had come and gone. Fox wanted to give me a bonus. He said he'd pay for a fishing trip to Qualicum or let me go to

Vancouver to cover the big track and field event. I took the fishing trip. The coho were running and they were taking surface flies. I was never too hot about track and field. The event I missed was the 1954 British Empire Games. Bannister, Landy, Peters . . .

By now my salary was up to a dizzying $75 a week and I needed every penny of it because I was married. Shirley was the daughter of a guy I played Senior B softball with. We moved into a three-room upstairs apartment in the pleasant Fairfield district and had our first child, Linda. I wasn't at the hospital when she was born and I was never permitted to forget about my absence. Linda was born around noon on a Saturday. I had worked my half shift and gone to McDonald Park to play football against the Royal Roads cadets. I was sitting on the bench when my father-in-law, Lloyd, came out of the stands to tell me I had a healthy daughter. I finished the game before going to the hospital. My bride was furious and my excuse, "But it was a playoff game," didn't win a point.

We moved to a nice rented home near the beach in Cadboro Bay and had our second daughter, Laura, and I figured, as a man with responsibilities and a fragile, 135-pound body, it was time to get out of contact sports, especially those blood-bath games with the Navy team. I had taken a hellacious battering from their defensive line in the first half of one memorable game. At half time I told myself the blocking would be better in the second half, or the Navy guys would tire. I went into the common toilet between the dressing rooms and saw two Navy linemen sitting on the concrete floor, passing a pint of whiskey back and forth. They grinned at me evilly. My kidneys dried up.

Navy had a terrific tackle and place-kicker named Doug Brown. We found out he had a heavy stammer and was touchy about it. When we needed a first down, I would come up under centre and stutter to Brown that we were coming right at him. He'd lose it and go offside, trying to get at me, and we'd get our first down. Brown turned pro with the Calgary Stampeders and won the Western Conference scoring championship with his place-kicking. But this was a very troubled man. It came out first when he sliced

quarterback Joe Kapp's face open with a broken beer bottle. Eventually he murdered a priest in Vancouver — knocked at the church door and blew him away with a double-barrelled shotgun. Brown was found unfit to stand trial and was institutionalized for life. I still see his face across the line of scrimmage, trying to get at me.

The last game I played was an exhibition against Annis Stukus's prototype Lions, the B.C. Lion Cubs, in the summer of 1954. They kicked the brisket out of us as we wallowed up to our ankles in mud and raw sewage at Brockton Oval. Someone threw three touchdown passes over my head. I figured it was time to pack it in and I threw my sodden boots into the storage room. When I went to get them a month later, there were long white hairs growing out of them. Thank God I hadn't gone face down in that Brockton sewage. I was too busy looking up at passes going over me.

We had a nice house, two adorable kids and my pay was up to $87.50 a week. I was looking forward to working at the *Times* until my retirement date. But then I got another of those telephone calls, like the one I got at the Land Registry Office from Bill Walker. This time it was Jack Richards, the sports editor of the *Vancouver Sun*. He had a job for me.

The *Sun* offer was irresistible. I'd get $100 a week with annual raises unless I turned out to be useless. A five-day work week with two weeks vacation. I'd handle the golf beat, write features and, since I had editing and layout experience, I'd rotate on the night and day desks. It wasn't thrown in but it was built in: I'd be working for the paper I had admired wistfully from a distance for so long, the paper that had a clear attitude of cheek and arrogance, that featured columnists like Jack Scott, Jack Wasserman, Barry Mather and Penny Wise. It was a gleamingly bright paper, partly because of the superb play it gave to pictures. I was very quickly taught the *Sun* code of picture use: if you have a first rate picture, run it big. If you have a second rate picture, run it really big. I was so anxious to work for the *Sun* that I almost grabbed Jack Richards by the lapel

through the telephone. My enthusiasm was not widely shared.

Les Fox, who had taken a chance at making me sports editor just a year earlier, told me I'd be lost at the *Sun* and would come crawling back to Victoria. Stu Keate wished me good luck and said he hoped we'd work together again some time. Shirley, who was pregnant again, was not happy at leaving her family but she didn't make a major issue about it.

Additionally, my dad was dying of cancer. After the shipyards, after a few years of miserable outdoor carpentry work that was hard on his health, he had landed the job of his life, as ship's carpenter aboard the CGS *Estevan*, a government lighthouse tender that did maintenance circuits around Vancouver Island, dropping off supplies and mail to the lighthouse personnel. Having been thwarted from joining the Navy during the war, at last he was at sea and as happy as I had ever seen him. A routine health check of the crew revealed that the ship's cook had tuberculosis. The other crew were ordered in for chest x-rays. My dad's x-rays showed some shadows on his lungs so they opened him up. There was no T.B. What there was was a swarm of cancer. They sewed him up and sent him home on disability leave. I told my mother that I was reconsidering the move to Vancouver. She told me in no-nonsense terms not to even think about turning down the chance of my lifetime unless I was damned sure that by staying in Victoria I could cure my dad. My dad died very bravely. My mother had to work so my dad stayed home alone, getting weaker. But he knew exactly what time my mom's bus dropped her off and he would have a pot of perfectly brewed tea ready for her and they would sit and talk about their respective days. I was glad that he had lived long enough to see his first two grandchildren.

But it wouldn't have mattered what anyone said. I was going. The *Sun* wanted me. I had my call-up to the big leagues. I was going to be a somebody.

It took longer than anticipated to wind up things in Victoria and to buy a home in Vancouver. I got weekly calls from Jack Richards reporting that "Swannie is getting upset" (managing editor Erwin

Swangard). I would learn that this condition was a daily fact of life at the *Sun*. But eventually, with cash help from my parents and from Shirley's grandparents, we bought a three-bedroom slab bungalow on a corner lot in Burnaby for $11,500 and made the move. We came over on the midnight boat, and as we passed under the Lions Gate Bridge at dawn, I realized something. I wasn't moving, I was coming home. All those years, Victoria had been my home-in-law. My real home was out behind those glittering lights around the harbour.

My cousin, Boyd Coates, and his wife, Lucy, met us and loaded us into their car. We drove out Kingsway towards South Burnaby. Just off the boat, in a car with a cousin on Kingsway . . . was this a restaging of my first arrival in Vancouver more than twenty years earlier? Not really. The streetlights were out and I didn't say anything clever or cute.

It was a long, thirty-five-cent bus trip in from Burnaby to work my first shift at the *Sun*, June 2, 1957. Shirley couldn't understand why I had to go in at 7. I must have forgotten to tell her that it was all night work in the *Sun* sports department. As I walked down Beatty Street, I was awed by the Sun Tower, a monster phallic symbol that had been the tallest building in the British Empire when it was known as The World Building. I got into the rickety elevator with another guy and went up to the fourth floor. The other guy also got off on four. We bumped shoulders going into the sports department. His name was Archie McDonald. He was just out of the University of British Columbia but had worked in the newsroom as a copy boy. He became, and remains, my best newspaper friend, an award-winning sportswriter and columnist, the guy who stuck the hideous nickname, Flyface, on me. When Archie won his first national sportswriting award, I sent him a note telling him how deserving he was and how happy I was for him. When he won his second award I sent him a note telling him to just fuck right off. It's that kind of friendship. When we celebrated the thirtieth anniversary of our first shift, I suggested to management that they buy us lunch. The cheap screws declined. When we celebrated the

thirty-fifth, Arch and I rented the Press Club and invited the new management as our guests.

But I'm ahead of myself. Barry Broadfoot was on the night desk when I reported in. He was there serving punishment for crossing the managing editor and he was sour about it. But I nailed the lead story that night and got my first *Sun* byline. Broadfoot, who was to become a good friend and a best-selling author, mumbled something that sounded like congratulations. I felt as if I'd got a base hit on my first at-bat in the majors.

Chapter 5

I like to think of the *Vancouver Sun* that I signed on with in 1957 as being a great oak-ribbed ship, pounding relentlessly through dangerous seas, its pennant snapping briskly at the tall masthead.

We're talking pirate ship here, with a half-mad, half-genius captain strutting on the quarterdeck, a gaggle of toffee-nosed officers demanding more speed, more booty and more lashes for the scurvy knaves of the lower decks, and a cut-throat crew with knives in their teeth, constantly ready to ram and board an enemy, or to mutiny and string the officers up by their greasy thumbs or to go ashore for a night of drinking and pillaging. Some days we did it all.

We blew the opposition out of the water at every opportunity, flew the *Sun* and crossbones and our name was known everywhere.

For openers, we were housed in a building, a roughly octagonal spire, that was designed for almost anything but the effective production of a newspaper. It has been said that someone, years ago, built an elevator shaft, abandoned it and someone else came along and wrapped an office tower around it. The fourth-floor newsroom was too small, so various departments were housed all up and down twenty floors, in little nooks and crannies where some of the writers began to display unmistakably batty behaviour, like princesses imprisoned too long in a castle tower. Drinking went on up there. There were bottles in the desk drawers, bottles in the urinal tanks. There was sex, too, I have been told. I don't know that first hand because I didn't get any, not in the old building, at any rate.

The newsroom ceiling used to creak from compressed weight some nights. That was because all the heavy machinery except the presses were on the floors above and we were fatalisticly resigned for it all to come crashing down on us, a murderous tangle of linotype machine, page stones, hot lead and printers who would warn us, with their last breath, that they'd file a grievance and hit the bricks if any of us touched type. The presses, thank God, were in another building a block up Beatty Street. We sent our half-round plates up there on a little underground railway and got page proofs and printed papers on the return trips. Somehow, we made it work.

It worked because our publisher-owner, Don Cromie, hired good people, paid them fairly and pretty much left us the hell alone. Cromie was a quirky guy, part mystic, part social gadfly, part supersalesman. Anyone with an idea for a perpetual motion machine could get an hour of Cromie's time because he figured such a device would avert a world energy crisis. When the Soviet Union launched the Sputnik satellite, Cromie sent a photographer a couple of thousand feet up in a propellor-driven plane to snap "close-ups" of the little ball in orbit. A free enterpriser by family genetic inheritance, he was tuned in to the likes and dislikes of the Vancouver business elite He left social issues to the socialists and made no apologies. When Jack Scott, the brilliant columnist whose heart bled through his shirts, complained once too often that the paper lacked a social conscience, Cromie said, "Okay, you run the paper."

So overnight, the most popular columnist the *Sun* ever had (he once wrote a column saying he was going up to Mountain Highway to pick blueberries: the next day the RCMP had to come in to sort out the traffic chaos created by hundreds of people who just wanted to meet Scott) became the editorial director. And he did it his way. He sent football columnist Annis Stukus, the former B.C. Lions coach, to Quemoy to interview Chiang Kai-shek and sent the dashing fashion editor Marie Moreau to Cuba to interview Fidel Castro when he came down from the mountains. Both assignments

worked brilliantly. *Sun* readers were particularly thrilled at the page one picture of brave Stuke, in a steel helmet, peering grimly through binoculars across the South China Sea at dangerous, Communist-dominated Mainland China, where the bad guys lived. Of course they didn't know that the tin helmet was borrowed from The Three Vets, that the picture was shot at Spanish Banks and that Stuke was looking at Point Grey.

Scott also sent eight male reporters out on the town with $20 each in expense money to see if there was street prostitution in Vancouver. The assignment was announced lavishly with an eight-column picture of the reporters, their backs to the camera to preserve their anonymity, framed against the Vancouver skyline. And then they hit the streets. It was preordained that they would find street sin and they did. What wasn't expected was that one reporter would disappear for three days, returning sick, dazed and demanding more expense money to pay for his shortfall. Scott also hauled me out of sports and gave me $25-a-week raise to write news side-features.

It all lasted nine months, the span of a good pregnancy, before Scott was replaced. He had made the mistake of being drawn into the office. As a columnist, he wrote from his West Vancouver home or from his summer place on Saltspring Island. Once, he was late getting to the ferry with a column that was to be handed to a mainland taxi driver and delivered to the *Sun*. He tore home, climbed into his rowboat, intercepted the ferry and handed the copy to a crewman. The column was delivered on deadline.

But by agreeing to work office hours, Scott made himself vulnerable to office politics. They got him, the Brutus faction in middle management claimed that Scott was a pinko and had hired an avowed Communist, the gentle Ray Gardner, as city editor. Scott was brought down and the great relationship collapsed in mutual bitterness. In his first day returned to managing editor, Erwin Swangard stopped by my desk and said, "Hey, Scott's folly, you know where you're going tomorrow?" I knew. I got sent back to sports.

During the fifties and sixties we put out as many as five editions a day, with new headlines, new pictures and updated breaking stories on killings, trials, bank holdups and whatever would titillate the prurient-minded. Beat reporters and street reporters filed their stories by telephone to our efficient rewrite desk, bossed by the brilliant Gar MacPherson, who stayed calm by pecking at a daily bottle of whiskey he had hidden in the men's room. Competition with the *Province* for a headline that would sell on the street that day was ferocious. Often the first man getting to a telephone would rip out the wires to prevent the opposition man from using it. Bonuses were paid for that kind of preemptive striking.

The tension needle in the *Sun* newsroom was constantly in the red, just short of boiler explosion. Telephones were ripped out and thrown. Typewriters and paste pots were smashed against walls. Reporters were fired just for being two minutes late. One sub-editor so loathed reporters that he handed them their assignments on the tips of a long pair of shears, to avoid physical contact.

Let me tell you about one day in the monkey cage. It was 1963. I had had a night off and had helped my Uncle Brice drain a bottle of very good rum. The telephone pulled me out of a very deep sleep near dawn. It was night sports deskman Skip Rusk calling to ask me why I wasn't relieving him. We had a contract agreement that a change of shift required one week's notice. I hadn't been notified, yet I was pencilled in the assignment book for the 7 A.M. shift. But it was no time to quibble. The Olympic Games were on and there would be a huge make-over from edition to edition. I told Rusk I'd get there as soon as possible and to cover for me because I figured someone's ass was going to bleed over the foul-up.

Desperately hung-over, I was stumbling into my clothes when my four-year-old daughter Linda came out, rubbing her eyes, asking why I was up. I told her I had to go to work. "Poor daddy," she said. "I'll make your breakfast." So I had to sit in a little chair at her little doll table and tell her how much I liked Kool-Aid and crackers for breakfast.

An hour late arriving, I tried to sneak into the sports depart-

ment. Swangard nailed me and demanded to know why I was so late. I told him the truth. He glowered. I knew that glower. "Tell Peters to see me as soon as he gets in," he said. When sports editor Merv Peters arrived, I gave him time to take off his overcoat, his scarf and his snazzy hat before giving him the message. He came back half an hour later and put his topcoat, scarf and snazzy hat back on. I asked him what was up. He told me he had just been fired and left.

I was mining through an open pit of news copy, trying to get all the Canadian Olympic results into the next edition, when Allan Fotheringham wandered in and began firing questions about my make-over. I conceded that he had been a terrific track and field writer before moving on to the photo desk but I couldn't handle him that morning. I said, "Foth, get out of here. I'll buy you a beer at the Lotus after shift but I'm up to my neck right now. Just piss off." He left, miffed. I went up to the composing room to supervise the make-over and my compositor said, "So Swannie fired Merv and made Foth pro-tem sports editor. Who'd-a-thunkit?" The printers knew the whole story before I did and I'd told my new boss to piss off. Later on, Foth told me I'd have a short career if I kept mouthing off. You could have a day like that at the old *Sun*.

The first full-tilt boogie I attended in my first year at the *Sun* was the annual Christmas bash that publisher Don Cromie threw for all the staff, except the dirty necks in the crafts unions. Imperial Rome never did it with more opulence and conspicuous decadence.

Liquor flowed like spring runoff. Aged deskmen and ad salesmen, crazed with Scotch, chased copygirls and switchboard operators all over the Commodore Ballroom. Dancers crunched dicarded lobster shells under their feet. Executive secretaries, dressed in hired gowns, performed credible can-can dances. Old resentments bubbled over into brief, clumsy fistfights. Cromie presented the keys to gold Cadillacs to the circulation manager and managing editor Swangard for keeping the profits up and the workers down. Swangard preened like a possum with a gold tooth.

But the highlight of the evening occurred when the sports department staff got up on stage and, with earnest Jack Lee backing them on drums, sang "Swannie, how we love ya, how we love ya, our dear old Swannie." I hadn't been around long enough to qualify for the choir and I couldn't believe what I was hearing. These guys had been hired by Swangard when he was the sports editor. They were his "kits," the closest he could come to pronouncing kids. But when he wasn't around, they cursed him in language that would peel wallpaper. With great patience, they had tamed a seagull by feeding it sandwich scraps on a windowsill overlooking Pender Street. They named it Erwin, they told me, because "it's either shitting or squawking." And now, flushed with Christmas and Cromie's booze, they were singing a love song to him, these tough cynics who took no lip from the toughest athletes and team managers.

I shouldn't have been surprised and I wouldn't have if the notion of tough love had existed then. Swangard had the power to split people into emotional shreds. Despise him today, you'd find yourself loving him tomorrow. He defined enigma with every rasping breath he took. I have been terrified by him, yet I have been moved almost to tears by some unexpected, undeserved kindness from Swangard. But lifetime terror leads love by a couple of converted touchdowns.

I came in off-shift one day to pick up my paycheque and do some shopping. I brought Linda and Laura, five and four, with me. They loved coming to the place where daddy worked. They crawled all over the horseshoe desk, jammed the typewriter keys and played with paste, paper and the big soft copy pencils. They were having a terrific time. I was reading my mail. Then Swannie walked in and spoke to me about something I hadn't done quite right. My daughters froze. We went shopping and they didn't say a word. We were almost back home on the bus when Laura finally asked, "Was that your master?"

He was intimidating. He didn't walk through the newsroom, he sailed across it like a ship of the line. Smaller people were swamped in his wake. Waves crashed long after he had passed.

Erwin was German. His father was a professor. Erwin fled to escape Nazism. He learned to speak English by attending movies in little prairie towns. He became a newspaper editor by sheer dint of will. He was a proud Canadian but part of him never forgot his German heritage. He was arrogant, autocratic, stubborn, bullying, unpredictable, and he was an empire builder. And we all courted him. We wanted his approval. We were proud to be his kits, but we wouldn't have admitted it at knifepoint. We preferred to turn Swannie-bashing into a cottage industry and, God, he did supply us with demolition materials.

From the Swangard file:

Swannie comes boiling out of his office and he's waving our sports pages like evidence in a murder trial. Sports editor Dunc Stewart is fifty feet away, but he can hear every word of an over-the-top Swangard rant. He calls me at home. "The Hun is walking around the news desk and everything out there has stopped. Apparently he doesn't like the lead on your football story. Looks like he's going to burst into flame. No . . . jeez, he's coming this way. Gotta go."

I waited long enough for any possible flames to subside and called Swangard. He said he didn't want to talk to me, that anything he had to say would be said in a memo. I went in that night in a state of near-death panic, expecting to be fired, and read the memo. Signed "EMS," it was mild and reasonable and suggested that I had missed the point of the game which was, in his opinion, that it had been a case of Calgary playing well rather than the Lions playing badly. But why the earlier performance for everyone? Just to remind everyone in the newsroom who might have forgotten that he was the guy in charge.

Another time, Swannie doesn't have an executive bathroom so he goes where we all go. He pulls off a handful of toilet paper and well, he scratches himself. He also explodes. He takes an armful of the scratchy toilet paper into his office and orders all his editors to drop everything and join him. He tells them he is sure he has uncovered a conspiracy to stick the editorial staff with cheap toilet

paper. He sends reporters and copyrunners to every bathroom in the building, including those used by the executives. They are ordered to bring back toilet paper samples. And so, with a deadline looming, all the people responsible for getting the paper out on the street are in Swangard's office, judiciously rubbing toilet paper between thumbs and forefingers, checking it for texture. The paper got out late but there was two-ply in the men's room the next day.

I'm going through a divorce trauma and living in a rented room with a hot plate. Swannie calls me into his office. He doesn't offer sympathy or advice. He says, "Kit, you're going to have money problems. I'm giving you another twenty bucks a week. Don't drink it up. And I want you to go to Winnipeg next week. Cover the Pan-American Games." I thank him for the raise and say, "But the Pan-Ams don't start for two weeks." He says, "I know when they start. Go next week. Have some fun. I don't want to hear from you for two weeks. Get out of here."

We have been on a short strike. It ends abruptly and we are called in to get a paper out immediately. As we pour into the newsroom, Swangard is standing near the door, glowering at us as if we had been caught playing hooky. He's ordering us here, ordering us there. He sees me but he can't remember my name. It's making him crazy. He points and snaps his fingers and jumps up and down in frustration and says, "Uh . . . ah . . . you, you . . . Sonny." Sonny? F'cryin' out loud, I'm forty years old. I've got five kids. I'm a senior reporter and he's calling me Sonny? It was days before I could pull myself together.

It's the night after the 1963 Grey Cup game, when Hamilton defeated the B.C. Lions. We are all in writing our game and dressing-room stories when Swangard bursts in like a cold weather front. Hamilton lineman Angelo Mosca had knocked the Lions star running back, Willie Fleming, out of the game with a heavy tackle on the sideline. Swangard has decided it was the dirtiest play in the history of sports, that it had crippled Fleming, and orders us to slant our stories from that perspective. He tells us we are going to "get" Mosca, the Hamilton coaches and the referees. We don't want

to do it. We all agree the hit was marginally late but not exceptional. I had tracked Fleming down in a Hastings Street bar two hours after the game and, other than a mild headache, he was fine. Since I'm writing the game story, I explain this to Erwin. We walk up and down a row of stills taken with a motor-drive camera, laid out on the floor, showing the play in detail. I see Fleming stretched out on the sideline. Swangard sees him two feet out of bounds. It's getting scary.

Our shop steward tells us that the only out we have is to write the stories as Swangard has ordered but refuse to have bylines on them. That's what we do. By the end of the next day, every newsroom across Canada is buzzing with the story of the mutiny in the *Sun* sports department. The mutiny story even buries the controversy about the game.

Years later, Paul St. Pierre explained it all to me. As he was leaving the stadium, Swangard had run into Cromie, who had been a guest in the royal box. Cromie told Swangard that the Mosca hit was the dirtiest play he had ever seen. Some of us suggested it may have been the first football game Cromie had ever seen. But it was enough to set Swannie off on a frenzy and embarrass the paper. According to Paul, who was editing the editional pages then, Cromie called in and dictated an inflammatory editorial in Paul's absence. Our venerable columnist, Bruce Hutchinson, was outraged, and phoned to ask Paul what the paper was sinking to when the editional pages wrote about "one leatherhead hitting another leatherhead on a football field." Paul agreed it was insane but Cromie, after all, was the publisher. Paul remembers that Hutch said, "Perhaps he's no longer qualified to be publisher." Pressure began to come from Max Bell in Calgary and Cromie was gone within months, resigning under pressure because he overreacted to one play in a crummy football game.

It took a couple of more years but Swannie had greased his own skids. Eventually the new publisher, Stu Keate, wrote and lost track of an undiplomatic memo suggesting that Erwin was getting too old and it was time to look for a successor. Swannie got a copy of

the memo. His lawyer filed suit for age discrimination. Swannie walked with $60,000, a year's salary.

One day in 1973, after I went to work at radio station CJOR, the station manager, Don Wall, told me, "Have I got a surprise for you. I've just hired your old boss Erwin Swangard as our news director." I almost fainted.

But we got along wonderfully well because Swannie didn't have any jurisdiction over me. He also steered some freelance work my way that permitted me to pay off all my drinking debts.

But he was still Swannie. After a few years of accidentally erasing news report tapes and trying to deal with radio egos, he decided to leave. He told me first. "You probably won't want to work here after I leave," he said kindly.

He's been gone a few years now but I still think of him, exploding all over the newsroom. I like to think I survived him. But if he walked into my den right now and glowered and asked, "Kit, are you writing all those old crap stories about me?", I'd lie. I'd say, "No, Swannie. No, honest." He intimidates me still.

Sportswriting is a pretty good dodge. It's about as much fun as you can have on a newspaper, next to owning one.

The travel opportunities are almost limitless on the big papers, the hours are predictable, the best seats are guaranteed at all the major events, and the free bar and buffet doesn't close until the janitor puts the lights out.

I recommend it as a newspaper apprenticeship but not as a career. It's good entry-level work, but who wants to spend his or her entire life listening to half-truths in stinky dressing rooms?

I don't think there can be a more pathetic sight than a sixty-year-old sportswriter, in his 1950s clothes, trying to pry a sensible quote out an arrogant, semiliterate athlete who earns $4 million a year stuffing a basketball down a hoop and then swinging from the rim like a diseased ape. Even worse, perhaps, is the look of blessing on that poor old dork's face if the athlete actually gives him something quotable, instead of telling him to bugger off, which is more likely.

The sports department has an important function as the cradle in the nursery. It is there that we develop our rudimentary language skills, get our literary legs under us, learn to stand upright. But we don't talk baby-talk all our lives and we don't stay in the nursery forever. We move up and out to explore the larger world, out there where the real issues live. If I were a managing editor, I wouldn't let any talented writer stay in sports beyond his or her thirtieth birthday. After that, I would tell them it was time to get serious about newspapering.

I enjoyed my almost twenty years of sportswriting, but I stayed too long. When I was pulled out to do a city column, I discovered with real fear that I didn't know much besides the infield fly rule.

I tried to do it well and I did take it seriously. And sportswriting was awfully good to me. In 1957, I arrived at the *Vancouver Sun* to take over the golf beat. I don't think I covered a single major tournament. The *Sun* had hired former B.C. Lions coach Annis Stukus to be their football analyst, a brilliant move because Stuke was, and remains, a beloved figure in Vancouver, and he had extensive journalistic experience behind him as a young reporter in Toronto. But in 1957, Stuke didn't want to be a leg-man. He wanted to write opinion pieces and didn't want to fuss with the daily nuts and bolts of the beat. We had tons of pungent opinion on our pages but we were being whipped daily by the *Province* on football news, signings, injuries, lineup changes. Something had to be done. Because I had played a bit, I was made the back-up football writer, the beat guy, actually. The timing could not have been more divinely exquisite. For those of you who weren't there, football and the Lions were the only topics of downtown Vancouver conversation in the fifties. Now, instead of writing little stories on amateur golf tournaments, which only the players would read, I was writing big stories about the Lions, helping set the conversational agenda. I had just come to town but my byline was becoming familiar. The football beat dug the foundation for my eventual elevation to columnist.

While we're all here, I can't let the opportunity pass to bemoan and begroan the state of sportswriting in the 1990s. I think we did

it better because we took more chances, expressed more opinion. The sports stories I read today are dressing room stories without real analysis. Maybe it's because every reporter has a tape recorder, slung on the shoulder that isn't carrying the portable Power Book. And that's why the game stories are so choked with quotes; the reporters turn on tape, the players babble into the mike and the reporter reels out a yard of taped quotes and calls it a game story. Well, it isn't. It's the players' and coaches' versions of the game and they aren't about to let themselves look bad.

In what other area of journalistic criticism are the performers permitted to make the judgement call? Does the music critic of the Vancouver *Sun* go backstage and ask the Vancouver Symphony Orchestra's lead French horn player, "So how do you figure you blew tonight?" Not bloody likely. The critic is expected to be knowledge-able enough to make up his own mind whether the soloist blew sweetly or fouled the air with a series of disgraceful clinkers. But repeatedly, in sports stories, we have Joe the quarterback rating his own performance. "I thought I threw good tonight. The inter-ceptions were just one of those things, you know?"

Thank you for this digression. I feel better.

Covering the Lions' nightly practices could be a bit of a chore but I did it cheerfully. I made all the road trips and I actually formed lifelong friendships with a few players, thereby disregarding that piece of advice Bill Walker had given me in Victoria. I had a certain respect for the workmanship of most players, for the guys who did it well for modest wages without making a big deal of themselves. Their attitudes, their simple dignity, are in glaring con-trast to the prancing, ego-swollen, self-aggrandizing fools who play professional sports today.

I guess what I liked best was the camaraderie of the *Sun* sports department. We were all reasonably young, making not-bad money and we liked each other. We were united in an undeclared war against management and it didn't take much to set off a victory party. We attended each other's weddings, celebrated the arrivals of children, helped each other through crises, played endless poker

games after our shift. Most Friday nights, we pooled our money and shared a lash-up dinner at the Ho Inn. The department's veteran, Roy Jukich, shared the secret of the best hamburgers in Vancouver. Not from the White Spot, but from Harry's Nightspot, out Kingsway at Schoolhouse Road. It didn't open until midnight, it was strictly take-out, but I have never tasted more succulent hamburgers. Harry was a cranky old former circus carnie, confined to a wheelchair by the diabetes that was eating up his legs. He dusted his grade A beef patties with a spice mixture that Heinz offered a lot of money for. If he was in a bad mood and there were only two of you in the joint, he might demand that you take a number before he served you. A kid pulled a knife on Harry one night and demanded his take. Harry reached up with one hand, pulled the kid over the counter and held him face down on the grill until he dropped the knife. Harry's was one of our after-hours hideaways.

At that time, the late Dick Beddoes was the duke of the department. A dazzling dresser, he was just as colourful a writer and he was endlessly patient and kind with the younger writers, holding writing seminars in the cafeteria, offering gentle, valid critiques of their stories to young reporters like Jack Lee and Mike Hunter. I didn't join the seminars. I didn't want his help, I wanted his job.

Dick could be breathtakingly funny. Years after he left us for the Toronto *Globe and Mail*, we sat together on the stadium roof at a World Series in St. Louis. He, of course, was immaculately dressed, topped off with a purple Borsalino. He was working to a tight Toronto deadline and, as I recall, with St. Louis down by two runs in the eighth inning and apparently out of it, he wrote and filed his story. The words were no sooner out of his hand than a Cardinal infielder named Julian Javier, from Panama, hit a two-run double to tie it. Beddoes's story was dead and he was personally affronted. As Javier slid into second, Beddoes bellowed, "Goddamn Panamanian, you killed my story. You make rotten hats, too." It was so, well, Beddoish that I almost wet myself.

But I guess what I liked best were the delicious absurdities of

sports, the little background pieces that never altered an outcome but which enriched my time on the sports beat.

Early sixties, the Lions are playing the Winnipeg Blue Bombers at home. The Lions have a young Canadian kid playing at defensive tackle and he is overmatched. A big, mean Bomber drives his helmet into the kid's midsection, really drills him. He hits him so hard that everything the kid has eaten the past two days flees for the nearest exit. His bowels are emptied, his pants are filled. He tries to gut it out, to act nonchalantly. But defensive captain Dick Fouts's nose twitches. "Who died?" he demands. The kid doesn't let on but Fouts traces the pungent smell to him. "Get out of my huddle," Fouts orders, "Get off this field." Abjectly, the kid goes to the bench. Defensive coach Jim Champion meets him on the sideline. "Are you hurt?" "No." "Well get back out there and don't let me ever see you trying to sneak out of a game again." The kid goes back out. Fouts makes him stand five feet away from the defensive huddle. Finally, after a punt, the kid gets to the sideline, tells the team doctor what his problem is, the doctor tells Champion, who apologizes and tells the kid to go to the dressing and take a shower.

Utterly humiliated, the kid is heading to the tunnel, head down and not walking too easily. He hears something. It is a small smattering of applause. It grows and grows. He looks up and everyone on that side of the stadium is standing, applauding him. He's one of their heroes and he must be hurt and they wanted him to know they love him. He keeps going, praying they never find out.

I'm in the Boston Red Sox clubhouse after a World Series game, at the back end of a mass interview of Boston pitcher Jim Lonborg. Lonborg has a tender elbow, which he must immerse in a tub of crushed ice after every game. Some of the writers think he is a malingerer. One of them asks, "Are you sure your arm trouble isn't all in your head?" Lonborg answers, "If it was, I'd have my head in this ice and you'd be interviewing my elbow." Jocks 1, Media 0.

Upcountry for a B.C. senior amateur hockey championship, I meet the trainer of the Nelson Maple Leafs, an amiable guy named

Bill. Bill also plays goal for an intermediate team. He is also the president of the intermediate league.

During a brutal intermediate game, an opposition forward spears Bill. Bill clubs him over the head with his goalie's stick. The referee throws them both out with match penalties.

Bill realizes he is between a rock and a hard judgement. Players who receive match penalties are suspended until the league president makes a ruling. Bill is one such player. He is also the league president.

"What did you do?" I asked breathlessly.

"I suspended the other guy two games and let myself off with a warning," he said.

As Don Cherry says, "Ya gotta love it."

Chapter 6

From time to time, I look back over my shoulder. Not to see if something is gaining on me. To see if I'm leaving a trail of horse-shoes.

As with any career, mine has involved planning, determination and talent. Each of those factors has contributed about .5 per cent to my rather long life in the newspaper business. The other 98.5 per cent has been luck, pure blind luck and freaks of timing. It's true, I swear to God it is.

I learned the elements of grammar and sentence composition because the Saanich School Board cruelly kicked a high school principal downstairs to teach grades seven and eight in the last year of his career. And Pop Garner, in one of his last acts of teaching, taught my class to parse sentences.

I got my first newspaper job because a young guy in the *Victoria Times* sports department decided he wanted to be a Mountie, resigned and left an opening for me. Had he not left when he did, there might not have been a position opened up for decades.

I got hired by the *Vancouver Sun* because they needed a golf writer. I was saved from that anonymous beat because they needed a back-up football writer, so I slid into the most prestigious beat on the sports pages.

In 1964, Stu Keate unexpectedly came back into my life. Don Cromie left the *Sun* and Keate was brought over from Victoria as the new publisher. I was, of course, delighted but didn't expect any personal impact.

On his second day in command, Keate called and invited me down to the publisher's office. I had been with the paper for seven years but had never been in that office. I had to ask the elevator man for directions. I stood there uncomfortably, but Keate put me at ease in a charming way. He said, "Let's sit over here and put our feet on Cromie's coffee table." It was a nice way of saying that he was now in charge and I was still his boy. He asked me why I was covering a beat when Jim Brooke was writing the column on the first sports page. The babbling Brooke, whom I heartily despised, was Swangard's boy. Erwin brought him in from Edmonton after our 1963 Grey Cup mutiny on the lower decks. Keate said, "Brooke's style is stale 1940s tabloid. I don't like it. Write a column tomorrow and I'll take care of the details." The next day I was the first page columnist. Brooke, who thoroughly despised me, was covering football.

And that's the way it has been my whole journalistic life. I didn't plan and make bold moves, I sort of hung around and got caught up and sucked along by changing tides. By treading water, I survived.

Opportunity knocked again in 1967. I didn't know it at the time, but the door was going to open, fall off its hinges and crush me flat.

My telephone rang in the sports department. It was Hilda Weston, Keate's private secretary who preceded him from Victoria.

"Boss wants to see you," she said.

"Be right there," I said. It was a long walk, the full length of the newsroom. I was aware that a few eyes were following me, but I put it down to inherent nosiness and the fact that there was a growing awareness, and resentment, of a Victoria Mafia in the organization. But I had no expectations of the call-in. I knew the gregarious Keate often got lonely in that huge office and he would occasionally call me in to hear his latest W. C. Fields anecdote or his Winston Churchill imitation. He did both voices superbly. But he was deadly serious and all business this time. He said, "I guess you know we have a problem with Wass." I did. Everyone in town did.

The paper had had a strike a couple of months earlier. Our saloon columnist, Jack Wasserman, the most respected, the most feared writer on the paper, made a terrible miscalculation. He predicted it would last six months. It lasted three days. But as a hedge against his prophesy, Jack had signed a contract with CJOR, Jimmy Pattison's radio station, to begin a daily morning talk show. The paper was struck on a Thursday. Three things happened the following Monday: we all went back to work; Wasserman began his talk show; all over town, billboards (Pattison also owned a billboard company) blared a half-true story: "The *Sun* is Down but CJOR Has Wasserman." Keate's blood could be heard coming to the boil.

Wasserman came in to write his column for Tuesday. He was told his column would not be running until he decided who he was working for. Wasserman's blood passed simmer.

They got together to try to work it out. Wasserman swore he was so well connected that he could do both jobs without either of them suffering. Keate just kept saying, over and over, "You can only work for one master. Make up your mind."

It was a Mexican standoff without the dusty street. Keate told Wasserman he was under suspension for breaching the exclusivity clause of his contract. On his lawyer's instructions, Wasserman brought in his column every night, as he had done for so many years. And every night the city editor buried it in a desk drawer.

So, yes, I did know what Keate meant on that December day. I thought he was going to tell me they had worked out a settlement. He didn't. He told me I was his answer. He wanted me to take over the saloon column. I wish I had said no, but my ego got in the way of my brain. Besides, Keate said, "I want you to be the new Mr. Vancouver." Well, come on, what stupid bee could resist that kind of free honey?

I really thought I could handle the job. I knew my way around Vancouver. I had drunk in the best bars, eaten in the good restaurants, gone to the clubs. I had even fed items to Wasserman and spent time over a few drinks with him. I had learned, from him and others, how he operated.

He worked sixteen hours a day, mostly on his feet, slipping from gathering to gathering with the same, simple question: "Got an item?"

I knew that if any of his contacts fed an item to a rival columnist, Wasserman would declare them "dead" for anywhere up to six months and they wouldn't get into the column until the time was served. I knew the deal he had with publicists. He'd print one plug item about one of their clients in trade for four items about non-clients.

I knew he got the best tables at the nightclubs, that he never paid for food and drink and that if he was hungry, he'd scarf food right off your plate. One restaurant had a goldplated fork on hold for him. It's said that he once absentmindedly ate half the contents of an ash tray.

It was a Vancouver tradition that readers grabbed their *Sun*, flipped up the front section to read Wasserman's column on the bottom of the second section. First they scanned it, to see if their own name jumped out in boldface. If it wasn't, they went back to the start and read, in terse items separated by three-dot breaks, all the gossip and speculation. The style of the column was to writing as Alphaghetti is to Fettucini Alfredo, but Vancouverites ate it up.

I knew that he knew more secrets than the head of the vice squad and that, while Jack Scott was the most popular columnist in the province, Wasserman was the most influential. He really could make or break careers.

And I was stupid enough to believe that I could replace him.

There were a number of factors I overlooked. I didn't know anyone outside the sports community. I knew the city but I didn't know its politics. I knew that a lot of people loved Wass and fed him, food and items. I naively expected them to love and feed me. They didn't. They didn't know who the hell I was. And I didn't know how much drinking was involved and how poorly I would handle it.

I needed the job and the pay raise that went with it. Shirley and I had divorced after sixteen years. I had moved out and was busting

my hump to pay support for our by then five kids, meet the payments on our big house in North Vancouver, and keep myself together. The divorce procedure went quite quickly but had, as later years would prove, something of a future celebrity presence. Her lawyer was Jack Volrich, an Anyoxer, ironically, who later became mayor of Vancouver. Mine was Al McEachern, a lawyer and rugby lover who went on to become president of the Canadian Football League and ultimately the Chief Justice of the Appeal Court of B.C.

I was given a week to prepare for my first column, which was to appear on Boxing Day. I'd have to write it on Christmas night. Paul St. Pierre, who was doing editorials, took me downtown to his club, bought me a beer and told me what it was all about. He said, "You won't be writing a column, you'll be putting out a newspaper within a newspaper. Your beat is everything: the movers and shakers, social tends, crime, politics, entertainment, the arts, everything that happens every day in the city." The beer was hardly wet enough to irrigate my parched mouth.

Two or three days before Christmas, I am crossing Georgia Street at Howe. Who do I see? The last person I want to see. It's Wasserman, in the doorway of the Hotel Georgia, and he has seen me. I knew he would be crushed at the loss of his column and I had no idea how he would react to me, his replacement. He grabbed me by my coat and said, "I want you to come with me." He hauled me up the block to where his car was parked, I got in and we started a very fast drive down Georgia, which was slick with ice. We were through Stanley Park and onto the Lions Gate Bridge before the thought crossed my mind that he might be taking me somewhere to kill me. I tried to look into his eyes for signs of homicidal insanity. We went up through that crazy maze of hills in West Van and pulled into his driveway. Jack held the stepladder while I put the star on top of his outdoor Christmas tree. Then we went inside and drank some Scotch while he gave me the names of a few contacts, wished me good luck and told me to drink lots of soda water. He said he'd had some trouble with booze but, "I've got a big body. I can absorb it. You're fifty pounds lighter than I am.

Watch it." And so I set out to become Mr. Vancouver. I didn't make it. I became the town drunk.

It's not that I didn't have a lot of fun and do a bit of good work in my brief career as a saloon columnist. I did, I really did. It's just that I took that saloon label as a mandate, as a vital component of the job description.

As well, I had the absurd notion that as an old-style newspaper-man I should be able to write and drink standing on my head. I tried it that way. I also tried it falling on my ass, and neither way worked. Most times, my average was pretty respectable. Nine times out of ten, I'd come back to the office between midnight and dawn after working my downtown traplines, write a readable column of between fifteen and twenty items, hand it in and go home to bed. One time out of twenty, I'd have the material but I'd have trouble typing. No problem. I'd find sympathetic helpers. I'd dictate, they'd type. There are a lot of former *Sun* copyboys out there who can say, with some truth, that they have written columns for the *Sun*. That I could get away with. What I couldn't fiddle and couldn't hide was that one night in one hundred when I simply didn't show up. I'd pass out somewhere, or wind up in a strange bed and there would be no column. The paper covered for me when that hap-pened. They'd run a little boxed insert where my column should have been, reading BOYD SICK. But those missed obligations piled up and the record of disgraceful irresponsibility still sticks to me like a rotten stink.

Some mornings I'd wake up late and in a panic, my mind blacked out. I'd phone my secretary, Ann, and ask her if I had writ-ten a column. If she said yes, and the column made sense, my reac-tion was typical of an alcoholic. "What a guy," I'd say. "Pissed as a billy goat but you got the work done." If she said no, I'd try not to think about it. I'd make my mind as blank as my recollection of the previous night. The colleagues who covered for me, the middle-management people who didn't call me on it, were unintentionally doing the worst thing they could do. They were enabling me to go

on shortchanging the paper. Only once do I recall getting a warning. Keate sent me a very plain-language memo. I read it and shuddered and stayed sober for a couple of weeks.

I guess what saved me was that when I was sober, I wrote a pretty good column. The three-dot format is one that was devised by Walter Winchell in New York tabloids in the 1930s. Maybe the best to ever do it is Herb Caen in the *San Francisco Chronicle*. You have to get the item, a snippet of news, a gutsy quote, write it in a way that crackles, and make it important by putting your own spin on it. One example. A few months after a federal election, I heard complaints that the veteran Liberal MP Art Laing was the last candidate in his riding to remove the ping-pong-table-sized campaign signs he had planted all over the riding. I wrote the item straight and then added the suggestion that since New Year's Eve was approaching, the general public might want to haul one of them home because, on New Year's, everyone wanted an old Laing sign.

It wasn't always that cutesy. One of the best things I did, and I stumbled into it, was to get an exclusive interview with the politician who spoke to no one exclusively, Pierre Trudeau. It happened during the fascinating 1968 Liberal leadership campaign. All the candidates came to B.C. looking for support. My colleagues, Allan Fotheringham and Marjorie Nichols, and I split them up and travelled with them. I shadowed John Turner around Vancouver and Victoria and got my crack at Trudeau in the Okanagan and Kootenays. Photographer Ralph Bower and I met Trudeau's plane in Vernon and were captivated by the guy's shy smile, the rose in the lapel, the Buddhist bow. As we barn-stormed with him we heard continual complaints from the members of the Ottawa press gallery about the lack of access to Trudeau, how he rejected their daily requests for one-on-one sessions and who in hell did he think he was? Being the new guy on the plane I didn't join the chorus of bitchery but I did ask that my name be added to the request list.

We were flying between Castlegar and Prince George, the grumbling media in the aircraft's front section, Trudeau curtained off in the small rear section. Someone had given Trudeau a six pack of

cheap Okanagan wine, a frothy rose. Trudeau accepted it gracefully but as soon as he could, he passed it to his handlers with revulsion. "Give it to the media," he said. A bottle was passed down my side of the airplane and I had it in my hand when I felt a tap on my shoulder. One of Trudeau's B.C. handlers, a guy I knew quite well, said importantly, "The minister wants to see you. Can you give him fifteen minutes?"

I was stunned. Was this a rib? I could hear a growing mutter as word passed among the senior press gallery guys. "The goddamn rookie from the *Sun* is going to talk to him." I got up, tapped Bower on the shoulder and hissed, "If this is legit, come back in ten minutes and get a picture." Bower was alert enough to see that I still had that damned bottle of plonk in my hand. He took it. I walked back. Trudeau's handlers had vanished. He was there all by himself. I said, "Good morning, Mr. Minister." A good enough start.

He said, "Mr. Boyd, I understand you have spent most of your career writing about sports. I'm interested in that area, in Canada's rather poor performance in international sports. I'm thinking of creating a ministry of sports and I'd like your opinion on why we have so few Nancy Greenes, so few Harry Jeromes, and what the government can do to help. I'd appreciate your advice."

Good God, not only was he speaking to me, he was interviewing me. The session stretched out to thirty minutes. Trudeau asked the stewardess to bring us drinks, Bower came back and took pictures. Trudeau was perfectly gracious but he evaded every question I asked him. I got a hell of a column even without answers from him. The only thing I did wrong was to underplay what might have been a warning to the Canadian electorate. In telling me about his own sports preferences, he said he liked squash, swimming, rock climbing and canoeing. He said he had no time for team sports. "I might want to go bowling at midnight. I have no time to sit around waiting for three other guys on a bowling team to show up." I used the admission and the quote but I buried it in the middle of the column. I should have used red ink and capital letters: The guy who wants to lead us isn't a team player.

The most fun I ever had with a prime minister was salmon fishing with John Diefenbaker. He was eighty-two years old at the time and retired from politics and the opportunity to fish with him at Campbell River came at the invitation of our mutual friend, Vancouver outdoors writer and author Mike Cramond. We fished and yarned and ate together for four days. And he didn't shake his wattles or harrumph at me once. We were there to fish and Dief took his fishing very seriously. He told me proudly about his personal fishing log: a seventeen-pound coho from a previous Campbell River trip, an eleven-pound steelhead from a B.C. river, a seventeen-pound Atlantic salmon taken on a fly, a six hundred-pound shark taken in New Zealand and a 159-pound marlin boated in the Barbados.

The weather was heavy and wet in Campbell River, not good for an old man's lungs. Cramond has always said that he can tell a man's nature by the way he handles a fishing rod. It was easy to see why he was so fond of Diefenbaker. Cramond and I met him at Painter's Lodge. We had just sat down for coffee after our floatplane arrival when Diefenbaker joined us, fully rigged out for fishing. He was impatient to get at it. He was blanked the first afternoon and not too happy that I, the pup of the group, took a spring and two feisty coho. The next day we were up and way in the black dawn. It was miserably cold but Dief, togged in water-proof clothes, really fished and really knew the Campbell River procedures. Even when using a rod-holder while he warmed his hands, his eyes never left the bobbing rod-tip, alert to the straight-ening of the rod that means a spring has mouthed the bait. He was rewarded: two coho, a plump pink, two dogfish and a cod. When we came in, he spun his fishing hat backwards, stretched and said, "This has been the most relaxing day I have spent in the last six years." He was clearly proud that he had spatters of fish blood on his hands.

At dinner that night, he ate heartily while telling us ribald stories about the famous leaders he had known: Churchill, Bevan, Queen Elizabeth, Eisenhower, Adlai Stevenson, King and Jack Pickersgill,

his favourite debating opponent. When word got around that the Chief was visiting, both Campbell River weeklies asked for interviews. Even though he was retired and vacationing, he gave them forty minutes in his cabin and supplied them with documents and reports from his portable files, asking only that they be returned in the morning. He peaked up to full thunder when asked about Trudeau's proposed constitutional changes. The years slipped off him and the patented Commons outrage took over. He was prophetic, too. "This is the most ominously dangerous thing our country has ever faced. This man is attempting to recreate the French Republic in Canada. He would strip the Queen of her power, make a puppet of the Governor General, alter the Supreme Court and do away with the Senate and the Privy Council. He would do this simply to divert Canadian eyes from a billion dollar deficit, a million unemployed and uncontrolled government expenditures." Some lion. Some repose.

A visiting American real estate man from Visalia marvelled that a former Canadian prime minister could go fishing unguarded. "I can't believe that I can have breakfast next to your former prime minister or talk to him down on the boat dock. If it was Richard Nixon he'd be walking around here four deep in FBI men."

On our way down to the Nanaimo ferry, we stopped at an Oyster shack at Union Bay. We were sitting outside, eating briny, raw oysters with toothpicks when a chunky man parked his Ford Ranger, ambled over, stuck out a meaty hand and said, "Gus McQueen from Calgary. How's she going, Chief?" It was as if one meets a former national leader slurping oysters at the side of the road every day. It was the particular charm of John Diefenbaker. It was also the particular charm of Canada.

The worst thing I did was go AWOL. I ran away to Atlanta when Martin Luther King was assassinated, April 4, 1968.

I was in a Vancouver bar with some guys, talking about it. One of the guys asked if I was going south to cover the story. I said no, it wasn't really my decision. A couple of martinis later, I asked

myself why the hell it wasn't my decision. I went to a lobby phone and called Swangard and asked if I could go to Atlanta to cover the funeral and the reaction. He scoffed at the idea, said he had the coverage well in hand, blah-blah-blah. I took offense at something about his reaction and the guys at the table sensed it. They goaded me, said if I had ten cents worth of guts I'd go on my own. Which is just what, after a few more on-the-rocks martinis, I did. The guys took up a cash collection. I called a travel agent and booked a flight and a room. I tore home, packed a bag, picked up my portable typewriter, told my roommate to cover for me as long as possible and, quite drunk, was on the midnight plane to Georgia.

At the coming up of the sun and the going down of the wheels in Atlanta, I was sober and sweating. Christ, what have I done? Swangard will take gas. But I had to go through with it. I caught a cab outside the airport. The huge female cabdriver caught my accent and asked where I was from. When I told her, she said I had every chance of some bad experience. Atlanta was ready to explode. She lifted a clipboard beside her and showed me a nickle-plated revolver. She told me that she and her twin brother, same size, worked the cab twenty-four hours a day and that if I wanted to stay out of trouble, they would be on call. They turned out to be a marvellous help, taking me to places I would never have got to, including King's house.

The problem was that Swangard caught up with me, got me by phone within twelve hours of my arrival and ordered me home. I said I was staying. He said there was no point in writing anything, I was suspended. I did write. I wrote my buns off. For two days, all my stuff was spiked. On the third day, after attending the emotional funeral, I wrote a story and a column that news editor Lionel Salt liked too much to spike. On his own, he ran both pieces. God bless him unto eternity.

When I ran out of money, I came home. On a miserably wet Sunday night, I got to the house I shared with two other recently separated guys at Forty-ninth and Angus. There was no one home. I contacted Swangard on his car telephone to say I was back. He

was not impressed. He called me everything but one of God's children. The scariest thing he said was, "This time even Stu has run out of patience. He wants to fire you. I'll try to save your job, but don't get your hopes up."

Totally demoralized, I walked down to the office in the pounding rain. I knew there would be a pay envelope in my mail box. I wanted to cash it in the morning so I could have a hearty breakfast before they executed me.

With the cheque and my piled-up mail, there was a familiar envelope. Office of the Publisher, it said. That's it, I thought. Stu has made his move. Two weeks notice.

I tore it open. I remember the text quite clearly. It said, "Denny: I cannot approve of your methods, but I am delighted that we still have people who show initiative when they get the smell of a story in their nostrils. Great copy! But there is a problem. Erwin has run out of patience and wants to fire you. Please make your peace with him. Bests, S.K." I looked up towards the invisible sky and whispered, "Thank you."

I survived that one, but the drinking was getting worse. I was miserably unhappy. Finally, after nine months, I went to managing editor Bill Galt, who had replaced Swangard, said I couldn't hack it, and asked to return to a sports column. He agreed. But I wasn't accomplishing anything. I was just taking what alcoholics refer to as "the geographic cure," hoping to control the drinking by changing the location of the drinking. It doesn't work. In 1970, the working and the drinking collided with finality. I had to make a decision. So I quit. I didn't quit drinking, I quit the job that was getting in the way of my drinking.

I came into the sports department late one night to do a column. I had half a bottle of rum in my overcoat pocket but not a single idea. I didn't know what to write so I wrote out my notice, went home and drank the rum. It was the start of a three-year binge.

Chapter 7

I quit. On a whim, without giving it any thought, I quit the only job I had ever wanted and walked away with a sad, foolish smile on my face.

I wish I could tell you why I did it but I can't. I was drunk at the time and I don't say that for a cheap laugh. I don't know what my thoughts were at that time. But I do know that the irrational decision was clear evidence that I had slipped two or three rungs lower in my plunge into alcoholic craziness, rather than descending them one at a time as I had been doing for several years. The best explanation I can give is that the alcohol devil in me was doing progressively more and more of my thinking, was jealous of the sober time that I was devoting to work. It told me to eliminate the work so that we could spend all our time together. It just seemed like a good idea at the time.

I gave up on the paper but the paper didn't give up on me, not without an argument. When Dunc Stewart, the kind, patient sports editor, got my resignation note the next morning, he took it to managing editor Bill Galt, who had already stretched the boundaries of tolerance, trying to get me back on track. He called me at home, telling me he wanted to tear the note up and forget the whole thing. I told him my decision was final, that I was sick of the newspaper business. Keate called me and asked me to meet him for lunch at the Marine Drive Golf Club. That scared me; I thought he might talk me out of it. I did meet him, though, and we had an uncomfortable lunch. He was sad and shocked, offered to do anything in his power

to make me change my mind. I told him that my plan was to wind things up in Vancouver and head down to Hollywood to take a crack at writing for movies, where the big money was.

Any group of recovered alcoholics would have a marvellous laugh at the comic familiarity of the scenario I was directing, certain in my mind that it was brilliantly original. I was only doing what every alcoholic has done at one stressful time or another. A rationale has to be created to explain the irrationality. I was protecting my habit, clearing out anything that got in the way of my drinking. And that move has to be made forcefully, without a shred of doubt in evidence. When the best friend you have is liquor, it is quite easy to eliminate all the other friends who don't understand you the way the booze does.

Apprehension was not a major factor in my taking that walk. Indeed, I may have saved Keate the messy obligation of having to fire me for cause. I had been working on mortgaged time for quite a while. I was coming to work sloppily and obviously drunk. I was pecking away at concealed pints in press boxes. And Keate never knew how close I came to botching one of his personal assignments just a few months before I quit.

Keate loved golf. So he felt he was doing me a grand favour when he asked me to fly to Victoria to cover a made-for-television match between Canada's George Knudson and the U.S.'s Al Geiberger, part of the very successful Shell Wonderful World of Golf. It was played at Keate's old course, the Oak Bay Golf Club, perched gorgeously on the edge of the Pacific Ocean.

It was a terrific match, Geiberger holing his tee shot from the elevated tee on one of the windswept par threes, on the way to a close match-play victory.

I spoke briefly with Knudson in the locker room. I had met him previously at the 1964 Masters' in Augusta, where he had been in contention until falling apart in the final round. (The Canadian sportswriters were unanimous in the belief that Knudson might have won that '64 Masters had he not gone out on the town the night before the final round with *Star Weekly* magazine writer Paul

Rimstead, a big league drinker.) I knew George had an expert's taste for good Scotch. "Ne Plus Ultra mist with a twist," was what he always ordered. So in the Oak Bay locker room he said he had a limousine waiting and that I was welcome to tag along to his motel. "The fare in Knudson's taxi," he said with a grin, "is one bottle of Scotch." I just happened to have one. It wasn't Ne Plus Ultra but it was Johnnie Walker Red Label, which passed the Knudson test.

I know we got to his motel but I don't know much more than that. I do know that I climbed hand-over-hand through a sticky fog to reach a telephone that would not stop ringing. I was in bed in my own motel. I was fully dressed except for a snazzy yellow cardigan sweater that had disappeared somewhere.

On the phone was Ron Loftus, the sports department night desk man who we called Pogo due to his bottle-shaped body and unflappable good nature. "If you aren't watching the clock, Den, it's 2 A.M. and I've got the pages filled except for two jeezly big holes for your golf story and your column."

Heart pounding, I muttered, "Sorry, man, but I'm just finishing up. I'll call you back."

I had the filled-in card in one pocket and a wad of notes in another. The notes on the match were quite legible. There were also notes on a rambling interview with Knudson that covered the metaphysics of golf, proof that there is a God, and a lot about the love George had for his wife and children. It was quite obvious that the track of the interview and the handwriting went down as the level of the two bottles of Scotch dropped. But from those notes, I managed to write a serviceable story and a pretty good column in an hour flat. I called Pogo and dictated both of them to him and he saved my job and my ass until that future night when I decided to amputate them myself.

Eventually, Keate realized there was no reasoning with me and arranged my settlement. With wages due, holiday time and my pension contributions returned, I put almost $6,000 into a bank account. I didn't go to Hollywood. I went on a binge.

I don't like the itemized, lip-smacking drunkalogues I hear at some twelve-step meetings. Too many of them are boastful, some sound almost nostalgic.

Let's just say that until the middle of 1973, I drank at a suicidal pace. I kept writing small cheques on my bank account to pay for my liquor, my rent and just enough food to keep me going. My cousin recalls dropping in to check on me and finding me sitting with three bottles of Tanqueray gin, one empty, one half empty and one in reserve. I was in Hollywood Sanitarium twice for dryouts. I suffered DTs and alcoholic seizures. When my bank account ran dry (and, unlike me, remained dry) I fielded enough freelance to survive. While working one day with my pal Greg Douglas, the Canucks' public relations director, I went into a seizure in front of his desk, hit the floor like a shot and split my forehead. An ambulance rushed me to St. Paul's Hospital, where I stayed for a week. I came back and finished the job and bought more gin.

As ugly and abstract as it is, I think you get the picture. I was sliding to hell in a green bottle, committing slow suicide. One alcoholic seizure can be fatal; I survived three of them.

In 1973, I quit.

It began with another of those fateful (there is no other word) telephone calls. A lady named Lil whom I had been seeing worked at the Grosvenor Hotel, which had the radio station CJOR in the basement. The station manager, Don Wall, remarked one day that he missed my column and wondered what I was doing. Lil told him I was doing nothing. He asked her to ask me to give him a call. I did and he invited me down to the station. Within an hour he hired me to write and read three sports editorials a day at more money than I had ever made newspapering. I knew I had gotten away with writing columns while I was drunk. I knew I couldn't get away with it on radio. So I had to quit. And I had help.

Just prior to getting that job, I was in the bar at the Top of the Marc, brooding into my gin and tonic, when I saw a female leg under the table next to me. I got down to check it out and met Robin. She was looking for a contact lens. We found it and each other.

Like my first wife, Robin was a redhead from Victoria. Like me, she was divorced. She knew nothing of my drinking habits until one day when she dropped in unexpectedly and found me completely wrecked. Instead of running, she literally packed me to her apartment and laid down some law. If we were going to have a relationship, I had to give up my first love. It was the first time that the idea of quitting drinking made sense to me. So I put the plug in the jug and started a new career in radio. The irony is that going without booze was a snap. It was radio that gave me fits.

I have heard a number of reformed alcoholics testify that they first realized they were getting sober when they began to remove the dishes from the sink before pissing in it. Well, whatever works.

For me, the first tangible evidence of change when I quit drinking in 1973 was creative energy, fiery bursts of it. I wanted to do things, dozens of things, right now. Mostly, I wanted to write. I wanted to prove to myself that I could still do it. I wanted to prove it to the Vancouver media market. And I wanted to make up for all the time I had squandered in drinking over the past four years. I didn't put myself through too much tortuous retrospection, but there were memories I wanted to put away in a dark room, with the door bricked up.

All the gin, all the scotch, had provided brief moments of false elation and short-term enlightenment. But the truth was as bleak and hurtful as the day-after hangovers: Through those four years I had been living in the lap of misery.

During one of my stays at Hollywood Sanitarium, an overburdened nurse asked me to help her restrain another patient, a truck driver, in what we called the Rubber Room. I literally sat on him for two hours while a strong sedative dripped into his arm through an IV needle. He howled and thrashed in delirium at the phantom images of seeing his best friend lose his brakes on a hill near Oliver and die in roaring flames. Later, when he was at rest, the dour, aristocratic owner of the place thanked me for the help. I thought to myself, "Great, I've finally impressed this snotty son-of-a-bitch."

Then he added, "You should know that when you came in, you were in worse shape than he was."

I was kicked out of a very nice apartment for setting my mattress on fire in a drunken stupor.

Hired to give a speech at a kid's sports banquet, I passed out in the men's room.

One time, perhaps seeking my behavioural level, I took a room at a seedy Granville Street hotel, me and my bottle of gin.

I was awakened by a heavy pounding on the door. I opened it carefully, expecting to see a fellow lodger who had smelled a gin spoor. But it was two uniformed policemen, grim-faced guys. They demanded my identification. I asked why. One of them said, "We were doing a routine check of the registry. You signed in as Denny Boyd. He's a journalist and he wouldn't be in a dump like this. Who the hell are you?" Instead of being humiliated, I was indignant. "I am so," I insisted and showed them proof. They went away, shaking their heads.

I almost died in Royal Columbian Hospital. My electrolytes were out of kilter and my kidneys were on the edge of failure. My mother was called over from Victoria.

It is unproductive to dwell on horrors like this, but their having happened, and the possibility of them happening again, can't be ignored. Better to put them behind you, but close enough behind you that they can look over your shoulder and say "Ahem" from time to time, just as reminders.

There is no question but that I owe my life to Robin, for giving me an attractive ultimatum, and to Don Wall, for giving me a job when I was a risky proposition.

So for the next five years I worked. I did my sports work at CJOR. I wrote a sports column for the *Georgia Straight*. (The graphics artist who illustrated and pasted-up my column was Doug Bennett, leader of the rock group Doug and the Slugs.) I freelanced articles to the *Sun*, just to let them know that I was able to make deadlines.

My new energy sometimes overwhelmed my common sense, as in 1973 when I agreed to write two books — and to deliver the

finished manuscripts on the same day. Taking on that double load was as insane as taking English 200 and 205 in second-year college.

The first book, for a small Vancouver publisher, was reasonably easy. It was to write a cookbook for single males, called *Man on the Range*, and based on some cooking columns I had previously written for the *Sun*'s food pages. The other book was much more problematic. It was to be the story of Vancouver's long, frustrating quest for a National Hockey League franchise, the building of the Pacific Coliseum and the team's first three seasons in the NHL. I did my research and had the book half-written when the Canucks' story changed dramatically: one of the American owners, Thomas Scallen, was convicted in Vancouver court and jailed for illegally diverting team treasury funds and issuing a false stock prospectus. I had to start all over again, but it was a terrifically more saleable story. I suggested to McGraw-Hill that, under the circumstances, the title should be *Pros and Cons*. Too inflammatory. They had recently been duped and discredited in publishing Clifford Irving's phony Hitler diaries and wanted to keep a low profile. The book was called *The Vancouver Canucks Story*.

Through the fall of 1973 I laboured on both books. Spring came. So did a gall bladder attack. I was in absolute agony one night while teaching a creative writing course at a west side high school. I went into the emergency ward feet first. The surgery some weeks later and the recovery put me on the disabled list for a few weeks. Finally, with an end-of-June deadline closing in, Robin and I took the five kids to a lovely cabin on Saltspring Island. Every day, from sunrise to spectacular sunset, I sat gingerly at a picnic table (the healing gall bladder incision still caused me to twitch with muscle spasms) with the cookbook manuscript to my left, the hockey book to the right and my typewriter in the middle and just pounded. I missed some glorious clamdigging but I got the two books whipped with a week to spare. I handed in the cookbook manuscript and had the hockey bundle, an original and three carbon copies, packed in a metal-edged box, ready for the mail.

Robin and I came home from dinner one night and I about

dropped dead. There was no sign of a break-in, but the box with the hockey book was gone. I think I sobbed. An hour later, Robin answered the phone. It was the booknapper and he had a deal.

Actually, it was Robin's estranged husband. They were on their way to divorce court and they were playing power games. Robin had gone to his townhouse and lifted a letter. He had come to our apartment and taken my manuscript. (He had managed to get his arm through the trapdoor where the milkman left the 2 per cent and unlock the door from the inside.) And now he wanted to make a swap. We agreed to meet him in the lobby of the Bayshore Hotel. From there we walked up Cardero Street to a white vw parked under the fifth chestnut tree from the corner. Robin gave him his letter, he handed me my manuscript, even wished me brisk sales. On our way home, I kept asking myself, "Did Ernie Hemingway have to put up with this kind of aggravation?"

My two publishers held a joint book launch. It was low budget. I stayed up all night cooking enough chili to feed all the invited guests. Both books sold about five thousand copies each and disappeared. I think I bought the last nine copies of the cookbook in a Granville Street book store, marked down to ninety-eight cents. As I paid for them, the clerk said, "Man, you must really like this writer." I still have a framed McGraw-Hill royalty cheque for $5.67. I never cashed it; it was worth more as a reminder of the difficulties of book-writing.

Every day I came to work at CJOR. I never really felt totally comfortable or properly placed in radio, but I knew I was lucky to have the job. I thought about newspapers, but I knew that, in that business, I had burned more bridges than the Russian army in the 1940 retreat to Moscow.

To my utter astonishment, quitting drinking was not difficult. I just did it. I didn't have any nervous tremors, no heaving stomach. My nerves did not twang like banjo strings and they didn't have to wrap me up in restraints, like Ray Milland in *The Lost Weekend*.

And I wasn't the least bit tempted to take a drink. My new employer, radio station CJOR, was in the basement of the Grosvenor Hotel which had a popular cocktail lounge in the lobby. Every day I passed that cool, inviting bar. I didn't go in. I knew my old self was in there, thirsty, and I didn't want to meet him. I walked past the bar five or six times a day and there was no magnetic pull. I had all I could handle, trying to learn radio.

My job, at first, was to write and read to tape, three two-minute sports editorials a day. The writing was easy. The reading was pure hell. Like every print person who jumps media, I wrote long, flowing, perfectly punctuated sentences. And then strangled myself trying to read them. I had to learn to write shorter sentences, with breathing spaces at regular intervals so that my untrained voice didn't peter out into a thin wheeze in mid-sentence. But with the kind help of the station's professionals, like Don Wall, John Barton, Neil Soper and Al Jordan, I began to catch the cadences and the timing, and things got better. In fact, everything got better.

Robin and I moved in together, into a West End apartment. And one by one, my five kids joined us. We had to rent another apartment on the same floor to contain the overflow. Very shortly, we rented, and later bought, a big house in North Vancouver with a stunning view and room for the seven of us. It was a hell of a challenge for Robin; she was less than ten years older than my oldest daughter and had never had kids of her own. On top of getting a risky husband and five instant kids, she held a responsible marketing job with Eaton's.

I was learning radio at the height of the talk-show wars in Vancouver. Wall, totally dedicated to information radio, had assembled a powerhouse of yackers. The same day I started, Jack Webster moved into the morning slot, having been lured away from the rival CKNW by a rich contract and the creation of his own satellite studio in Gastown. There was Ed Murphy in the afternoon, Pat Burns at night and the late Chuck Cooke on weekends. They were a fascinating lot, quick thinkers, bellicose debaters, fuelled by egos

that burned at the heat of liquid iron. Wall made a shrewd move, putting Webster in a studio across town; his ego grating against that of Burns would have imploded the entire building.

I did my six minutes of opinion and spent the rest of the day trying to figure out these guys. I was listening to Webster one morning while driving in and noticed that he sounded down. The Oatmeal Savage, as we called him, was thin gruel. On a whim, I stopped in Gastown and visited him. He was glum because he had no guests, no audience to play to. But my presence kicked him up a notch. Then two Vancouver cops dropped in for coffee. Now Webster had a live audience of three people and his program took off. I was to learn that insecurity is a daily crisis for all radio personalities.

Burns was the undisputed father of talk radio in Vancouver and had, in fact, patented the term "hot line." Possessed with a brilliant mind, a memory like a blotter, hard-right conservative views and a voice like lump coal rumbling down a steel chute, he brought in the advertising revenues that fuelled CJOR long before Webster was hired. Burns didn't have to worry about playing to an empty studio, he had to worry about constant death threats and CRTC ultimatums. And he was really a sweet, friendly guy, except when he had an open mike in front of him, or had drunk his lunch. One afternoon, Neil Soper grabbed me and said, "Come on, Denny, we have to get Pat out of there." Burns had been on air for five minutes, four of which had been filled with commercials on orders from Soper, who had realized Pat was bombed. Burns stood barely five-foot four-inches tall, a fact that amazed people familiar with the voice but meeting him for the first time. It always amused me that when he was shaking the air, his feet weren't touching the studio floor. This made our evacuation job easy. Soper took one arm, I took the other and we lifted him up and out like a piece of lightweight furniture. Burns didn't protest when we took him to his office, and I was proud of my part in averting a disaster. Then I was horrified when Soper said, "Denny, get in there. You have to go on for him. And don't tell anyone that he's drunk." I settled in front of the microphone — my feet didn't touch the floor either — and saw

a note that I was to talk to a maverick Liberal MP in Calgary. I had never heard of the guy but I faked my way through the interview and then opened the lines. Every caller wanted to know where Burns was and why the pismire from the sports department was talking politics.

I secretly hoped to stay with 'OR long enough to get my own talk show, not because I felt I was born for it, but because I knew that was where the big money was. But filling in for Burns was not the way I had planned to ease in.

The year before I joined the station, Jimmy Pattison, the multi-millionaire owner, had bought a hockey team, transferring the franchise of the Philadelphia Blazers of the new World Hockey Association to Vancouver. The NHL Vancouver Canucks were doing dismally and Pattison, with no previous experience in sports, figured a new team in a new league would run the NHL out of town. God, was he wrong.

At Pattison's request, I attended one of his board meetings and learned how big business works. He was grilling some of the Blazers executives he had inherited. At one point he asked a young marketing man, "Ron, how are we doing on that that discount tick-et deal with McDonald's?" Ron said, "Oh great, Mr. Pattison. I talked to Arnie at the Fraser Street store and he's really interested." The temperature in the room dropped forty degrees. I swear frost formed on the walls. Pattison's senior directors looked at the floor, waiting for the death sentence. Pattison swung around in his swivel chair a bit and then said, "Ron, this is the Jim Pattison organiza-tion. We don't talk to Arnie. We talk to my very good friend George Cohon, the president of McDonald's of Canada." Ron was on his way back to Philadelphia by the end of the week.

The Blazers, a collection of retreads and overpaid rookies, were a bust, but they were an interesting experience. This was at the height of the free agency movement, when players in all profession-al sports were throwing off the iron chains of contract bondage and were auctioning off their talent to the maddest bidder. Pattison asked me to find him a public relations mouthpiece who could

handle the hostile Vancouver media. I couldn't find anyone so I took the job myself, splitting my work day between the radio station and the team offices at the Pacific Coliseum. Joe Crozier, an experienced NHL coach, was brought in as coach and general manager, and a clash was inevitable. Crozier was old-school, adopting the martinet methods of his mentor, Toronto Maple Leafs coach Punch Imlach. Imlach and Crozier had had the big hammer: just one big league and a lot of minor leagues where recalcitrant players could be banished until they learned to follow orders without question. It had worked for years and made players not much better than indentured slaves. But now there was an an alternate league, players were hiring agents, money was falling out of the sky and players of dubious talent were learning to tell coaches to go pound salt up their asses.

I lasted one season. The Canucks killed us by putting together a superb team that won its division and sold out 15,300 seats for every home game. The Blazers were lucky to draw six thousand no matter how many tickets we gave away. One night, before a late-season game, Pattison frowned at me and said, "Denny Boyd, you're my friend. How could you let me get into the hockey business?" A few weeks later, Crozier called me into his office and said, "Lad, they're panicking downtown. Two guys are on their way out here to fire you. Don't give the bastards the satisfaction." I didn't. I wrote out my notice and went back to radio full-time. During the off-season, Pattison moved the franchise to Calgary.

But the great radio adventure wasn't over. Wall phoned me one morning and asked me to come down to the station.

He and Soper, the program director, had a bunch of program tapes piled up on a desk. Wall said they were going to turn Vancouver upside-down and that I was to be the tosser.

The tapes were from a Los Angeles talk show called "The Female Forum," hosted by a purring-voiced guy named Bill Ballance. What the program was was a sex clinic. You know, just the run-of-the-mill stuff like mutual masturbation, multiple orgasms, impotence, foreplay, having it off in bathtubs filled with lime jello.

The show was a sensation in L.A. Wall was sure it would go over in Vancouver. He needed a new voice. Mine. It would run from 12:30 to 3 P.M. There would be a nice raise in it, lots of technical support, plenty of lead time to make sure we got it right. All I could think about was having my own talk show. I should have given more thought to the sex-in-the-jello warning, or that Greater Los Angeles had 120 radio stations and that any kind of programming could find a niche in La-La Land. I should have twigged when my wife laughed herself breathless when I told her I was going to do a program about sex problems.

They told me nothing could go wrong, that Vancouver was changing and was ready for frank talk about sex. To make sure the first show got off fast and hot, we salted it. We primed all the young women in the station to call in to brag or complain about their lovers' performances. That got us through the first forty-five minutes. After that, a silence so complete I could hear traffic going by on Howe Street. And that was just the first day. On the second day, the organized hostility began. I was called a sexist pig, a filthy degenerate, a threat to women, children and possibly to small farm animals. People who couldn't get through to me jammed the phones at Pattison's head office, demanding that I be taken off the air. At the end of the first week I couldn't hold food down. Wall said we were right on course for terrific ratings.

The program lasted six months. We tinkered and toned it down but the program was doomed. Vancouver simply was not ready or willing to talk about sex in anything but discreet whispers. Fortunately, my belly gave us an out. I had to have surgery to remove an inflamed gall bladder. While I was out, CJOR scuttled the program.

It had nothing to do with work but Robin and I split. There was no bitterness, no name calling, no attempts to damage each other. It just seemed that the odds against the marriage caught up with us. The age difference was a major factor, as were our dispostions. Robin was ambitious, hard driving, wanted to set goals and acquire things. I was revelling in mellowness and unwilling to set targets or

make long-range plans. And the challenge of Robin becoming step-mother to five teenagers overnight was just too daunting and caused too many domestic arguments. When pushed to take sides, I inevitably took the sides of the kids.

We worked out the divorce sensibly, split the cost, sold the house and shared the proceeds. I bought a townhouse in North Vancouver and became a single father. It seemed to work out for everyone.

The next damned thing to go was my pancreas. All that gin I had drunk in the preceding years had turned the poor thing to a lump of nonfunctioning stone. I was always tired, constantly as thirsty as the Gobi Desert. I blamed it all on work stress. But at breakfast one morning, former Canucks hockey coach Hal Laycoe watched me pound down two glasses of ice water and two of orange juice with my eggs and said I had all the symptoms of diabetes. Blood tests proved it. After getting the results, my doctor called me and said, "You're the walking equivalent of a raspberry popsicle. Get yourself to Vancouver General as soon as you can. I've booked a bed for you."

I said, "I'll get there as soon as I can but traffic is heavy."

He bellowed at me over the phone, "Call a cab. Don't even think about driving. You could go into coma."

They put me though more tests, pulling blood and muttering numbers that didn't mean anything to me. And the next day, the Hospital Employees Union struck the hospital, removing all the nonmedical staff. The Teamsters honoured the HEU picket line so no fresh food was coming in. The bad news was that we had to make our own beds and most meals were thawed hamburger patties and Kraft Dinner, not the wholesome food needed to regulate my runaway blood sugar levels. The good news was that I was inside a struck hospital and was able to feed CJOR's newsroom with the only live coverage from the inside. On one report, I complained about the food shortage. My friend Hy Aisenstat, owner of the best steakhouse in town, had a complete steak dinner smuggled into me. The next day there were two picketers outside his restaurant.

On the fourth day, I answered my bedside phone. A very weary

94

voice said, "Mr. Boyd, this is Dr. Edwards and I'm calling to apologize. Usually we give new diabetics a complete indoctrination program. But with all this, the clinic is closed and I hope you'll bear with us."

I told him, "I can understand that but the nurses have been great. Yesterday I injected an orange and today I gave myself my insulin shot, right in the arm. Tonight I'm going to shoot it up in my butt."

He said, "That's terrific and that's a good way to start. But you realize that it will be more complicated when you're released."

"How so?" I asked.

"Well, perhaps they haven't told you yet but after the first few shots, you have to start injecting the insulin through your penis."

I fairly screeched. "Is this a rib? Who the hell is this?"

His voice got hard. "Mr. Boyd, I have a struck hospital. I have no clinic staff. I can assure you I have no time for jokes."

I apologized and asked him to go on. My knees were up around my ears.

"You'll be surprised. It won't hurt that much. The new needles are very sharp. Just make sure you space the shots, and try to keep a straight line. Eight shots should do it."

"Eight shots," I croaked. "Space 'em, straight line. And after that?"

"After that we'll send a piccolo player around to teach you to pick out a few tunes on it."

It was then and only then that I knew I had been had by Vancouver's most notorious practical joker, the diabolical Murray Minions. That night, my blood sugar reading was off the chart. The nurses couldn't figure out why.

Chapter 8

Maybe I would have bluffed and blundered my way through an entire career in radio (many have), but I rather doubt it. Not blessed with a sonorous voice nor the quick glibness required for talk radio, I reached the peak — actually the foothill — of my radio potential quickly. I knew I would not get better. I knew I had written some good sports editorials but I didn't know if anyone was listening. I had the creepy feeling my mark on radio would always be summed as "the guy who did the kinky sex show." The money was still alluring, and Wall was one of the greatest men I ever worked for, but I was restless. I needed another of the improbable alignments of the stars that had rescued me in previous years. What I got was not a miracle, it was a tragedy. I didn't get another momentous telephone call; this message came by radio.

I was driving home in North Vancouver one night when I heard a CJOR news reader lead off with the announcement that Jack Wasserman was dead. He had collapsed, in a tangle of microphone wires, with a massive heart attack while giving a witty speech at a roast for logger-politician Gordon Gibson in a downtown hotel ballroom. Wass was dead before he hit the floor.

I went home and wrote a tribute to Wasserman and dictated it to the station. I was in shock. So was the whole town. Jack was fifty years old. But his were fifty roughly used years. He smoked heavily, drank too much, slept too little, ate like a foraging wolf and was kept in a constant state of stress by the demands of his five-a-week column. A few weeks before his death I had met him back-

stage at a fund-raising telethon. He told me then that he had suffered severe chest pains during a recent trip to Montreal. "No big deal," he said. "Keep it to yourself."

After a decent interval, I began getting calls. Friends, old colleagues from the *Sun*, suggesting I apply for the job. I made no such move but I received a note from Stu Keate. He said he had heard from enough people that I wasn't drinking, said it was "time to come home," and suggested a discreet lunch. Keate didn't want it known that he was shopping the job around so he suggested we meet outside the office, at one of his favourite Italian restaurants. It just happened to be the place where all the wheeler-dealers who ever made Wasserman's column met to eat, drink and tell lies. And when we slipped into our table, there was a gabby radio reporter at the next table. The next morning it was reported on radio that I was returning. But in fact, we didn't have a deal. Jack Webster had taken me aside, told me I was dealing from strength and told me to price myself accordingly. When Keate asked me what I wanted, I said I wanted what I was earning at CJOR, a car and a secretary-researcher. I was ready to toss out the secretary demand, but it was on the car that Keate balked. He said it was against company policy, but I knew that most Pacific Press executives were given company cars. CJOR had provided me with one and I wasn't about to buy my own just to change jobs.

Negotiations bogged down. Finally Keate suggested an intermediary, my old pal Fotheringham, the reigning star of the paper who had been my Monday replacement the first time I tried a cityside column. Keate said, "I think you two old jocks can settle what you and I can't."

No chance. Fotheringham met me for an early morning breakfast at the Hotel Vancouver. Foth was not well, sleepless and faintly green with hangover. He had just arrived on an early ferry from Victoria and told me he had been up all night drinking scotch with Bill Bennett, and that "Bill wouldn't go down." I felt actual pity for him as I watched him push aside most of the cheese omelet he had ordered. I learned a good lesson that morning: never try to dicker

with the hung over. When I reiterated that I wanted a car he snapped, "The *Sun* isn't a radio station and we aren't asking you to deliver a milk route for Jimmy Pattison."

I have no idea what he told Keate but very shortly I received a gracious letter from Keate, offering the car and the requested salary for five columns a week, four on the news pages, one on the food pages. When I told Don Wall, he said he was delighted for me.

And so, in January of 1978, I walked back into the *Sun* newsroom. I wasn't expecting a round of cheers but the silence of the place stunned me. The *Sun* had installed its first newsroom computer system. The clattering sound of Underwood typewriters was gone, replaced by the puny clicking of computer keyboards. It meant that I would never again hear the machine-gun racket of Jack Brooks, the paper's best deadline writer, hammering out a story against the clock, ripping out the pages and bellowing, "Copy, f'Christ sake." The *Sun* didn't have copyrunners now, it had Systems People. And one might hear a frustrated reporter ask piteously, "Would someone get me a systems person, please. I'm locked up."

My first walk through the newsroom was revealing. I saw this big, handsome kid with a mop thatch of curly brown hair, shambling along in turned-down yellow rubber gumboots. That was the film critic, Jamie Lamb, a young wizard soon to take the Ottawa bureau post. There was a chubby little guy in wrinkled chinos and a Grateful Dead T-shirt. That was Vaughn Palmer, the rock critic. Eventually he would buy a couple of neckties and become the *Sun*'s legislative columnist and the most respected political commentator in the province.

I didn't realize it at the time but the *Sun* was a paper in decline. Its demographics were chilling. The average reader was fortyish and no one under thirty was buying the paper. Management's relations with the trade unions, a militant bunch, were poisonous. In his fourteen years at the *Victoria Times*, Keate had never had a strike. He knew most of the printers and pressmen by name, spon-

sored an annual golf tournament for all the unions and poured whiskey generously for all the dirty necks at the prize giving. But Pacific Press was a whole new game on a whole new course.

Additionally, Keate was nearing the end of his watch, his health was failing and, like many men in power, he hadn't trained a successor. It had been assumed that Fotheringham would eventually succeed to the publisher's chair. But in his post-retirement biography, *Paper Boy*, Keate wrote that despite his personal fondness and respect for Fotheringham, he did not see him as executive material.

That had been borne out when Keate gave Fotheringham a new title on the masthead, Senior Editor. The job gave Foth a nice office just down the hall from Keate, lavish expense accounts and a hand in recruiting and hiring new staff. Foth made a meal of it.

For all his personal charm — and I loved the man — Keate had a thin skin and he could go ballistic if he thought his geniality was being manipulated. While Fotheringham was in eastern Canada, Keate was told his senior editor was telling people he was the equivalent of the *Sun*'s assistant publisher. Keate didn't even bother to check out the report. He ordered the presses stopped in midrun, a costly, emergency-only step. On orders of the publisher, a pressman in oily overalls climbed into the middle of the presses with a hammer and a cold chisel and sliced Fotheringham's name off the masthead.

But they had been through too many good times and too many stressful times to stay mad. Fotheringham joined the rest of us in the newsroom, teary-eyed, October 31, 1978, as Keate said goodbye and introduced our next publisher, Clark Davey, who told us how eager he was to work with us.

On his final day, I asked Stu what he would miss the most. He said, "In my office, even with the carpets, I could always feel the vibration come up through my legs when the presses began to roll. I'll miss that."

I did a post-retirement story about him and asked him to name the six most memorable people he had met in his long career. He

gave me six. But he kept phoning to add more names. When the list was up to eighteen, including a Haida totem pole carver and a Victoria cab driver, I had to ask him to stop calling.

He wrote about his retirement with his typical wit and grace, and what he wrote in *Paper Boy* is as poignant today as it was in 1978:

"When I started in the craft, some of our veteran reporters were still writing their stories in longhand. Now, forty-five years later, we were totally into electronics; the newsroom looked like NASA Control in Houston, with about one hundred video screens and black cables snaking across the floor.

"I thought of the dreadful time when we had a numbing crash of the entire computer system and all the stories disappeared from their screens — indeed, from the host receivers. In the elevator I met one of our electronic whizkids and asked him what happened.

"He replied — and I quote — 'Our infrastructure suffered an improbable interface.'

"As an editorial boffin I wasn't about to let him get away with it. So I fixed him with a flinty stare and murmured, 'Surely you are guilty of an elliptical solecism.'

"Wordlessly we stepped off the elevator.

"There, in microcosm, was the problem at Pacific Press. We spoke to each other but in strange, incomprehensible terms.

"It was clearly time to go."

Go he did, and in cruelly short order the Boss was dead.

It is romantic nonsense, the notion that newspaper people bleed printer's ink. They don't: when hurt, they bleed hot, thick, mortal blood. And this truth was never in more grisly evidence than in the period of the late seventies and the mid-eighties, when there was blood splattered on newsroom walls all across Canada. It was a terrible, but instructive, time to be in the business.

I bled when Stu Keate, my long-time patron, left the *Vancouver Sun* in 1978, wearied of fighting for jurisdiction with the absentee owners, weakened by the onset of Parkinson's disease. But mine

was an emotional bleeding, not life-threatening. I wiped it up and got on with things.

Clark Davey, Keate's successor, surely bled inside, despite his bravado. Davey was an Easterner, a swashbuckling former managing editor of the Toronto *Globe and Mail*, a Conservative party supporter parachuted into a west coast paper that traditionally backed the Liberals. He was loud and vain. For some reason, *Sun* staff nicknamed him Waldo, but I found him to be a good newsman and, more importantly, a standup guy who cared for and protected his employees.

But within twelve hours of Davey being introduced to the news staff, the paper was shut down by a strike-lockout impasse. It was the fifth strike in ten years. We were out for eight destructive months, which bled away 25,000 subscribers. We had barely regained that number from a four-month shutdown in 1970. During another strike-lockout in 1994, my colleague Nat Cole counted up the down days of his lengthy career and estimated he had been idled a full calendar year.

Davey, while obsessed with expensive reader surveys, was a good choice to succeed Keate. Keate had brought a maturing to the *Sun* which, under Cromie, had been a raucous, juvenile and self-obsessed paper, more concerned with how many drunks had been arrested the previous evening than in what was going on in the nation's capital.

We survived the strike, though the faint, pink scars are still evident in hostile labour relations and lost circulation. Many of our colleagues across Canada were not so lightly wounded. In Victoria, my old paper, the afternoon *Times*, and the morning *Colonist*, which had been publishing independently since 1858, merged in 1980, even though both were profitable. The merger cost fifty people their jobs and seemed indefensible.

The Calgary *Albertan*, the *Winnipeg Tribune*, the *Ottawa Journal* were all closed down. I had old press box pals at all three papers.

I had asked Davey if I could get away from the three-dot gossip column format. I was tired of nightclubs and the celebrity scene

and wanted to be able to write full-length essays on a single topic. I was increasingly interested in all levels of politics and wanted to express some opinions. Davey endorsed the idea to my satisfaction. I was getting older, I was a step slower and I figured the switch to regular hours would be good for my health. What did I know?

I didn't bleed but I surely did quiver some on June 19, 1980, when I had my heart attack.

I had turned fifty the previous evening. It was something I had fretted about for at least six months. In fretting, I created a self-fulfilling prophesy, or what I prefer to call my Catch-50 bind. I was unduly aware that my predecessor, Jack Wasserman, had dropped dead at fifty. I was occupying his old column space. I was coming up fifty. Therefore, I would have a heart attack at fifty. And, be damned, I did.

The week before my birthday, I was so stressed I took a week off and drove to Vancouver Island. My disc jockey friend Fred Latremouille offered me the use of his fishing shack at Bamfield. I stayed there one night, didn't like it, locked it up and drove to Courtenay and the B.C. Lions' training camp. But nothing would get me out of my morbid funk so I came home. My ravishing red-headed friend Lesley Zahara, one of the two best friends of my life, insisted she was taking me out for my birthday dinner, and since I'd had no other offers, not even from my five kids, I agreed — but said I wanted a quiet night. We went to the Fish House, where I was rotten company, disregarding Lesley's concern that my diabetes would not like the two-inch slab of Key Lime pie I scarfed down for dessert. Lesley suggested we go to Viva, the trendiest nightspot in town, for coffee. We did and I got blindsided. There were three hundred people there, friends, colleagues, people I regularly wrote about, all five of my kids. I hadn't expected a thing.

Among the fine gifts I received was a talking bird of some kind — the label on the huge cage said Boyd's Boid. Around 3 a.m., I took the bird home and, since it seemed terrified, I placed it in my bedroom. The damned bird muttered all night and I didn't sleep. I felt rotten the next morning but headed for work around 9:30. I

felt the grab when I was halfway across Lions Gate Bridge.

It began as a twinge on the left side of my chest. I actually looked down and said, "My God, I'm having a heart attack." The squeeze on my chest increased. I was sweating and having a hard time getting a deep breath. And there I was in the middle of the goddamn bridge with nowhere to stop. I got over the bridge, through the causeway and was driving up Denman Street, wondering which hospital I should head to, indeed, if I could make it to a hospital. Insanely, I actually tried to remember what I had heard about the food at the downtown hospitals. Finally, I headed for St. Paul's and parked my car in a lot across the street. I momentarily fished for meter change but decided, if you want my car, too, God, you can have it. At the emergency desk, I stood behind a lineup of the previous night's casualties, drug ODs, knife, fight and car victims. The nurse in charge, practising good triage procedure, looked past their visible wounds to me, in my suit, shirt and tie, and asked what my problem was. "Chest pains," I croaked. She hit a button and within minutes I was stripped and on a gurney, plugged into various monitors. The intern in charge told me he didn't think I had had an attack yet, but one might be on the way. He had me medicated and questioned me closely on what I was feeling. And then it came.

It was a miocardial infarction, a dreadful name classifying a blowout in the heart's casing. Being medicated, it came with the absence of any pain and I can only describe the sensation as a great rippling, hall-of-fame orgasm. Then it was into the Intensive Care Unit, an oxygen breather and a deep sleep. The nursing staff had promised to phone the paper to say I wouldn't be in, and asked for the names of three other people who should be informed. I gave the numbers for Lisa, my third-oldest daughter, my lady friend Lesley, and my best male pal and roommate, Andy MacGregor. Every time I woke up, one of them was standing at the foot of my ICU bed. Lisa wept, Lesley tried to apologize for letting me have that Key Lime pie, and MacGregor asked me what in hell I was doing. "Resting, you twit," I said.

In a week I was in the cardiac ward, walking around, looking

forward to my first substantial meal. It came at lunch, a piece of fried liver. Just as I was about to get into it, Lesley and Robin both walked in, creating a tension that might have been entirely in my mind. On top of that, I had the CKNW noon news on and sportscaster Al Davidson, based on God knows what reporting, announced, "There's bad news from St. Paul's Hospital. Denny Boyd has taken a turn for the worse and I ask you to pray for him." Hell, I was fine. I just wanted to get my teeth into that liver.

One of my first visitors had been Davey. He roared into my room like a formula racing car, assuring me no one would fill my column until I was ready to come back and advising me to get a hinged butter-box. He had had one made to order and he used it every day as a step-up exerciser to build up his cardiovascular system. It folded flat and fit into a suitcase. Before I got out, I made friends with the intern who had talked me though the attack. His name was Tom Perry, a young man deeply concerned with nuclear disarmament and environmental protection. One night, when he was bone weary, he complained about the chronic shortage of equipment at the hospital, particularly on the night shift when many facilities were locked up.

"We need another blood centrifuge, another good microscope and we really need a portable ECG machine. We could buy them second-hand for around $3,000. A guy with a job like yours, maybe you could go public and get the money donated."

I didn't go public, I went sneaky. I called up a lot of high-rollers, told them they were prime candidates for coronaries and how would they like it if they died because of an equipment shortage. I scared the poor wretches so sufficiently that they ponied up $16,000 which were donated to St. Paul's.

There were three postscripts to the heart attack story.

Dr. Tom Perry ran for the New Democratic Party in a subsequent provincial election and won a seat in traditionally Social Credit Point Grey in a massive upset. Eventually, he became minister of the environment. I used to wonder what I would do, how much I would owe him, if he ever became premier of the province.

I had to take four frustrating months off work while my heart healed. I walked miles, banged tennis balls off walls, ate boring food. A week after I returned, I went to the press library to ask for my own picture and bio file. It took them half a day to find it. It had been placed in the obituary file, standard journalistic practice.

Years later, Robin was hit with chest pains on a Saturday morning. She took a cab to St. Paul's and was hooked up to an ECG in the emergency ward. Her attention was caught by a small brass plaque on the side of the monitoring machine. It said, "Donated by Denny Boyd and Friends." She shrieked down the corridor, "Is this someone's idea of a joke?"

Chapter 9

Maybe if I had been born and raised on the Canadian prairies, where the winters are cold enough to freeze the nuts off a steel bridge, I would have know more about the properties of ice. But no, I was born in the coastal sunshine and rain and was quite ignorant as to how ice froze.

From my decision day in 1973, I stayed sober the hard way, the white-knuckle way. I followed no program, had no support. I just didn't drink. I did it myself and told myself that it was working because I neither drank nor had any inclination to. I failed to add the word 'Yet' to those declarations. I had friends who were in twelve-step programs, but I thought they were complicating a rather simple course. If they asked me if I wasn't creating a risk, I told them about ice. I would say, "In the beginning, it was dangerous, but I'm getting safer and safer every day. See, it's like walking out on a frozen pond. The ice is thin near the sides, but the farther you go to the middle, the thicker the ice gets. I figure I'm out far enough that I'm pretty safe."

My physics and my airy sense of security were both wrong, both doomed. After eight and a half years I hit thin ice and fell in. God, it was cold, shockingly cold. Knocked the breath and the cockiness and the naivete right out of me.

I thought that my piled-up days of dryness had created a cure, that I was under control, that a couple of gentlemanly drinks, taken with care and respect, couldn't hurt me. Nice theory, but applied to the wrong person. I went right back to piggish drinking. I piled up

my car and spent the night in jail. That happened on a Saturday in February, 1982. Like a good Christian boy, I rested on Sunday. First thing Monday morning, a policeman delivered a couple of summonses to my door. I was so low I would have had to reach up to touch bottom. Primarily, I wondered if I had finally blown the job. I absolutely dreaded the prospect of having to walk into the publisher's office, across that long expanse of carpet, stand in front of his desk and lay it all out, detail by guilt-ridden detail. But Clark Davey relieved me of that ordeal. He called me. He said, "I hear you had an exciting weekend." I muttered something like, "You have no idea."

With a mixture of briskness and joviality and not a tinge of accusation, he said, "Look, Denny, don't worry about the car. We have lots of cars. Don't worry about the charges. We have good lawyers who will take care of them. And don't worry about the job. Good columnists are hard to find. We have a lot of time invested in you and we want to protect that investment. Would you mind if I popped over to your place in the next hour?"

This was astonishing. The publisher wasn't calling me onto his carpet. He was coming to me. He arrived and asked me if I had any idea what had caused me to slip. I said that I obviously hadn't learned my lesson. That seemed to be what he wanted to hear. Davey said, "We have a place down below the border where we have had some success in sending people with this kind of problem. We pay the shot. But it's five weeks and there's no point in going unless you stay the course. Are you willing to go?" The prospect of getting out of town, away from my problems, away from curious telephone calls, was irresistible. I said I'd go.

Later, the *Sun*'s promotions manager called and told me he'd pick me up in an hour. He told me to pack a small bag and lock up my apartment. Once on the road, he surprised me with his knowledge of the place we were heading for. Then he told me he was a recent graduate. He had done his five weeks, had shaken off a serious pill addiction and turned his life around. He was almost evangelical, so much so that in my soul-bruised condition I was almost

tempted to jump out of the speeding car. In Kirkland, Washington, north of Seattle, we pulled up at what looked to me like a pleasant little junior college. And before we went inside, I got a walloping surprise. Jogging laps around the grounds I saw one of the *Sun's* copy editors, an old friend. He had been there for a week and welcomed me.

Being sober by this time, I had no trouble filling out the reams of application papers and medical background. I was given a physical that might have gotten me into the army. They even took hair samples to check for mineral deficiency. Finally, I was issued a pair of pyjamas and was sent to bed for three days, not for punishment, but to wait out the normal detoxification period while the last traces of alcohol in my system burned off.

When I was allowed to join the general population, I found that Alcenas Hospital was, indeed, like school. I was issued a copy of what Alcoholics Anonymous popularly calls "The Big Book," other books and pamphlets, a notebook and a daily schedule. We attended classes, lectures and small group sessions six hours a day and were expected to take notes. We made our own beds, were assigned sweeping-up duties and took our meals cafeteria-style according to individual diets dictated by the medical staff. Every instructor, nurse, lecturer and supervisor was qualified by having overcome an addiction problem. They had heard all the stories.

One wing of the facility housed juvenile drug abusers who stayed for up to three months. That led to some strange encounters. One day, in a small group session, a young guy went into a screaming fit, ranting that he wanted to leave. He then fell to the floor convulsed with racking sobs. He pulled himself together and told the group that three years earlier he had murdered his best friend, kicked him to death over a drug deal. He said he had been living in such a hell of guilty torment since then that no amount of liquor or drugs could heal his conscience. For the rest of us, who were just looking to get some sobriety, it was hard to deal with. Was the story true, or a drug hallucination? Were we under any obligation to report the crime? Later that day we were called back

to an emergency meeting and asked if we were troubled by the kid's revelation. The group vote was that the outburst deserved some of the dispensation of the confessional box and that any legal decisions were up to the administration. The kid finished out his stay. The group supported him in formal sessions but gave him a wide berth otherwise.

Quite honestly, I can't separate what I learned at Alcenas from what I have learned in my subsequent twelve-step program. But my time there did erase any corrosive guilt I may have had over my addiction, propped up my self-esteem and underscored the acceptable fact that I could never drink again. I did my five weeks and left Alcenas feeling not like an idiot or a moral degenerate, but like a person with a disease for which there is no cure but which can be kept in permanent remission with proper care.

I got close to a number of my fellow inmates, most of them from the Seattle area. Like so many Americans, they liked the idea of having "the Canuck" around. As each of us graduated, we signed our Big Books and promised to stay in touch. Of course, we didn't. The only thing we had in common was alcoholism. There were poignant moments, too. I saw some of the American guys with their families during visiting days, the wives playing the victim role. Then, as the weeks passed and the program restored their self-esteem, the guys began to talk about how they were going to take charge, to be responsible and to make the decisions that had been thrust upon their wives during the drinking years. Some of the wives plainly resented this attitude. There seemed to be a smouldering grudge that, "You got sober for these people but you never got sober when I asked you to." I wondered how long it would be before these guys would be back.

Lesley and my old *Sun* sports department pal Jack Lee drove me back to Vancouver, and I got ready to return to work with a lot of enthusiasm and just a little bit of fear.

I had sent a message to Clark Davey saying that when I got back, I wanted to make full disclosure, to write some columns about the entire experience. Davey wrote back giving me a free and

enthusiastic hand. He wrote, "If you want to spend next week re-establishing your contacts, we could highlight your return in Saturday's paper, say, and carry your columns through Monday and Wednesday. By then you should be back in full swing. If you want to start sooner, that would be no problem for us. It will be great simply to have you back. I'm sure you know there have been plenty of calls wondering when your column will start up again." Hardly a scolding return for the prodigal son. As I have said, Clark Davey is a standup guy.

I did write three columns on my experience and I tried to be honest about it. (How else was I going to explain my absence from the paper for five weeks? Say I'd been in Maui?) In the first column I admitted to being an alcoholic. I wrote "I have a disease that will kill me if I do not control it. The disease is alcoholism and I tell you this with no shame. To apologize for my inability to handle alcohol would be as foolish as to feel disgraced because my diabetes cannot tolerate refined sugar. I did not choose to become an alcoholic. I am the victim, not the cause, of my illness. Sick people do not become alcoholics; alcoholics become sick people."

In the second column, I wrote about my surprise at finding out that, in addition to being an alcoholic, I was also pill-addicted. Four days into my stay at Alcenas, I began to experience some frightening symptoms, quaking, sweats, chills, sleeplessness. The medical staff put me though a second session of examinations but couldn't pinpoint my problem. Finally, one nurse asked me if I used prescription drugs. I told her I frequently took sleeping pills, thirty-milligram strength. And that was the answer. I was going through drug withdrawal from what I believed and millions of Canadians and Americans still believe is a benign, nonthreatening form of medication. I have not taken a sleeping pill since that time. I don't trust the little buggers any more than I trust whiskey.

In the third column I outlined the treatment program at Alcenas and expressed regret that British Columbia did not have such easily accessible treatment.

In retrospect, I am not so unequivocally sure that long-term, in-

house treatment is the only way to get sober. It is fiercely expensive: my treatment cost the *Sun* $6,000 in 1982 dollars. Many Americans are covered by Blue Cross insurance which is not available to Canadians. And what the five weeks led me to was a lifelong commitment to my twelve-step program, which is available to everyone at no cost at all.

The response to those three columns, in volume, was staggering. And ninety per cent supportive. For many people, living with an addiction or with someone who had one, it provided the courage to face the problem, to talk about it, rather than hiding it as a family scandal.

I'm not the perfect Alcenas alumnus. In the next couple of years, I slipped twice for brief periods. The twelve-step program tolerates such slips, but sends you back to square one in the snakes and ladders game of sober time. You start over again from Day One and pile up the days, one at a time. On January 3, 1995, I celebrated twelve years of absolute sobriety. The program works when you work at it.

I tell myself and others that staying sober is like being on permanent parole. It is taking a course that only losers graduate from. And I'm still going to classes, still reading the book. To function, I need insulin twice a day, pasta once a week, Italian sausage once a month and a twelve-step meeting once a week.

Accepting that I will never drink again for the rest of my life is not so tough, not when it pretty much guarantees that I will never throw up on my shoes again, one of the lesser reasons for getting sober but one that, curiously, remains vividly in a sober mind.

Before you ask, and we get involved in a dialogue that will leave you dissatisfied and me breathing hard, let me tell you that I don't know why I drank the way I did when I had so many other safe alternatives. I don't have a clue. Rogue gene, lame morality, clinical depression, personal and professional frustrations, residual brain damage from getting clouted over the head with my own cap gun by that belligerent neighbour-girl in Anyox? I don't know.

If you think that is strange, perhaps even irresponsible, let me tell you further that I don't need to know. This is information that I do not need. In fact, having the answer might be dangerous; it might make me think that now that I 'have the answer,' I have the right to drink again. I don't want that.

The human species has been drinking for about six thousand years. In Isaac Asimov's *Chronicles of the World* the late author points to 4,000 B.C., by which time people in the Middle East had learned about the fermentation of grape juice and soaked barley, so that wine and beer were beginning to come into use. Undoubtedly, these drinks became popular because they induced intoxication and, in moderation, made people feel good. Asimov points out that such beverages were important in another way, though the early drinkers could scarcely be aware of it. Alcohol tends to kill micro-organisms, so that drinking wine and beer was safer than drinking water which might be contaminated with human or animal waste.

Asimov fails to mention another highly significant consequence of man's first discovery of fermentation. Until that time, the humans of six thousand years ago were nomadic, constantly on the move, seeking new supplies of food. But when they discovered the pleasure of grapes and fermented barley and hops, they stopped roving and put down crops of these reliable products. They coalesced into groups to plant; they waited to reap. These gatherings became the first permanent social groups of what would lead to permanent cities. The tribes that boozed together stayed together.

That surely is a positive aspect of drinking alcohol that must be stacked tall against all the undeniable social ills that the demon unleashes on those who handle it poorly. But despite countless, costly and often windy research reports, we still don't know much about alcohol, why nine people can drink it sensibly with no personal consequences, but it will clamp on to the tenth person like a rat's jaws and ruin his or her life.

That's not so surprising, really, because the two groups most involved in alcoholism can't be trusted. One of my former doctors, a widely respected general practitioner and a damned nice and

112

conscientious man, couldn't believe I had a chronic problem. He thought I had too much pressure in my job and in trying to support a family of seven. So he gave me tranquilizers and sleeping pills to help me cope. He treated one drug with another drug. He was a member of two or three generations of doctors who had received exactly three hours of lectures on alcoholism during their seven years of university training. He would have been better qualified to help had I come to him suffering from yaws. The medical establishment is marginally more enlightened now and there are, in most major cities, specialists who treat nothing but alcohol problems. But there are still doctors who deny alcoholism as a disease and treat it as a nervous disorder.

The bigger problem is, of course, the drunks. They're all liars who cunningly defy any effort to accurately chart or profile them. They have to lie. They are protecting a friend.

One of the best studies of alcoholic behaviour I have ever read was written by a Canadian, Art Hill, in a 1974 edition of *Canadian Literature*. Hill was actually doing a character analysis of Malcolm Lowry's magnificent novel, *Under the Volcano* comparing the drink-controlled behaviour of the consul, the protagonist, with the ruinous drinking of the tragic Lowry, who lived for a while in North Vancouver. Lowry suggested as his epitaph, "Malcolm Lowry/Late of the Bowery/His prose was flowery/And often glowery/He lived, nightly, and drank daily/And died playing the ukelele."

In probing Lowry, I think Hill tapped into the alcoholic lifestyle and mindset as accurately as anyone has. Hill writes: "It is one more affliction of the alcoholic that he is always ashamed of his drinking. This is why, drunk or sober, he maintains the fiction that he could drink moderately, and surely will next time. He does not, ever, consider stopping until he faces the fact that moderation is not within his power.

"One device the alcoholic uses to enforce the self-delusion that he doesn't 'need' the drink is the tactic of spurious indifference. Given a drink after a period of abstinence (of any length) the

alcoholic simply delays drinking it. Deferring the moment of consumption supports the belief that it will be voluntary."

I used to do that. Shaking in the morning, I used to phone a liquor delivery service to bring me my scotch or gin. Every second I waited peeled skin off my nerves. Then, the knock at the door. It was here! But I would put the bottle on a table or a shelf and just glance at it fondly for a half hour before starting on it. I was convinced this separated me from really serious drunks. That's another characteristic of drunks: they all think they are unique, that the common criteria don't apply to them and therefore no one can possibly understand them. They resist all available treatment programs because "It wouldn't work for me." Then, if they ever get to an Alcoholics Anonymous meeting and listen to speakers or read the stories in the Big Book, they are astonished. They feel they are reading their unauthorized biographies. They ask, "Jeez, how did they know. . . ?"

Hill writes with laser accuracy: "No one who is not an alcoholic can ever understand the alcoholic's need to drink. He does not understand it himself, but he knows what it feels like, something no outsider can know."

A broken leg, a ruptured appendix, pneumonia, they all send out clear and unmistakable 'Alert' messages that there is a problem and where it is. But alcoholism is the only disease that convinces the victim that he doesn't have it. That treachery, combined with the drunk's pathological lying and the lack of diagnostic or treatment savvy in the medical profession, is why there is so little documented awareness of the lethal nature of what too many people believe is nothing more than a social problem. Alcohol abuse is one of the top five killers of people of all ages. And even the available figures on "alcohol-related" deaths were suspect. How many unexamined traffic deaths were caused by a drunken driver, too mangled to be tested? How many multiple deaths in house and apartment fires are caused by a passed-out drunk with a burning cigarette?

Alcoholics think they can keep drinking and things — health, work, moods, relationships, business — will get better. They don't.

114

They get worse. And then they die. Denial gets them just as surely as the toxic effects of the alcohol do. Winston Churchill liked to boast, "I have taken more out of alcohol than alcohol has taken out of me." True, perhaps. And possibly denial. Dylan Thomas, the brilliant Welsh writer and two-fisted boozer, frivolously described an alcoholic as "Someone you don't like who drinks as much as you do." Thomas was in his grave, as pickled as a gherkin, by the age of thirty-five.

But Seneca the Younger was onto something as far back as 60 A.D. when he wrote, "Drunkenness is simply voluntary insanity."

So, failing to find anyone who understands them, damned few who sympathize with them and no prescription pill that cures their addiction, a fortunate fraction of abusive drinkers will fetch up at the door of an AA meeting. They will be nervous, full of doubt, riddled with angst about being found out. At his own sincere request, I took a flashy, theatrical, successful Vancouver businessman to his first meeting. "What if somebody recognizes me," he fretted in my car. "It'll be all over town by morning." I said, "Just try to be inconspicuous." He missed the irony. He was wearing a white suit, white shoes and a white, scalloped sports shirt opened deeply enough to show off a glittering medallion the size of a ham platter. The first three people who greeted him at the door recognized him and told him how welcome he was. He got over his initial concern and stayed gratefully in the program until his death.

The twelve-step program of AA is the only thing I know that works outside of complete, white-knuckle, self-administered abstinence. My pal Don P., thirteen years in the program as I write this, once signed up for a controlled-drinking program (surely an oxymoron for alcoholics). It permitted him a certain number of drinks every week, providing he kept a scrupulous log of when he took them and under what circumstances. It worked for a while, then it failed hugely. Don P. went on a three-month bender. He woke up in a strange hotel room with no idea where he was or how he had gotten there. Looking out a window he saw a sign on a building that said "City of Quebec." "Thank God, I'm still in Canada," he

breathed. Wrong. He was looking at the City of Quebec Hotel in London, England.

AA, which provides long-term sobriety to about 20 percent of the people who come to a first meeting, is widely misunderstood. Too many people think it is a religious organization, because they hear about a Big Book and a Serenity Prayer. AA is not founded on religion; it is based on spirituality. Religion comes from without. Spirituality comes from within. AA searches for that flickering spark of pride or courage or dignity that usually exists in the worst falling-down drunk. It blows on that spark in a group effort. It doesn't preach: it teaches. It doesn't forbid or demand. It suggests a program of recovery. Alcoholics are notorious for resenting being told what to do. The program is taught by the only people that drunks will trust — other drunks who have put their drinking on hold. AA does not judge, does not condemn. There is no dogma, no penance. There are are no thou-shalts or thou-shalt-nots in the twelve-step program. It asks that the seeker go to meetings and not drink between them. There is no constitution, no president, no board of directors, no roll call, no executive and no dues, other than what goes into the collection basket to pay for the coffee, which is consistently vile.

It lasts forever, renewable daily. You cannot sign up for a six-month crash course. There are no report cards or personal evaluations. Those who stay get a cake and handshakes on the anniversary of their last drink. To those who come to one meeting and say it's not for them, it is suggested that they give the program a fairer chance, say ninety meetings in ninety days. Many do. Those who choose to go out are given a full refund on all the problems they brought in.

Somehow, it works, sixty years after two hard-drinking American men, a doctor and a stockbroker, started it in 1935.

I often think that if Moses had brought down the twelve Suggestions and if AA tried to sell the ten Commandments, there would be a lot more Christians and a lot fewer recovering alcoholics.

116

Chapter 10

Getting sober after a long bout of drinking is like waking up in a strange room. There is serious dislocation.

There are panicky questions: Where am I? Who am I? What happened? How much trouble am I in? Then, a deep breath, an immense feeling of relief. It's okay. I'm not in trouble. I know where I was every minute last night. Everything is under control. The sun is shining and I think I am going to enjoy it.

In fact, there will even be gratitude for the blessing of a full night's sleep. For the first year or so, recovering alcoholics usually wake up every three hours, like a nursing infant. The unrest is caused by parts of the body calling room service to complain. A lot of organs and nerve clusters have become used to being inundated and soothed by regular arrivals of alcohol. When the delivery stops, they get owly and call the brain to complain, "Hey, where are the goodies we ordered?" It takes a while to convince them that liquor is no longer on the menu and that they might as well settle down, stop grumbling and catch some sleep.

Getting back into the swing of work was not a great problem. In fact, I clung to the job like a shipwreck victim to a floating hatchcover. The return to the unforgiving discipline of a five-times-a-week deadline was just what I needed to focus my mind on being responsible to myself, to my family and to my employer. And I had help everywhere I turned.

My colleagues at the *Sun* and all the editors were first class, welcoming me back, encouraging me, never belittling me. On the odd

occasion when I dropped into the Press Club, they lined up to buy my first soda water.

I had the support and affection of the two best friends I ever had, my long-time buddy and soul brother Andy MacGregor, and the wonderful Lesley Zahara. You don't need a ton of friends when you have two of such quality.

I met Andy in 1966, when I returned from an out-of-town assignment and found him sleeping in the third bedroom of a house another friend and I were renting in Lower Shaughnessy. I turned on the light and this enormous guy sat up in bed and said, "Hi Den. I'm Andy. I'm your new roommate." Momentarily, the encounter scared hell out of me. But then he produced a bottle of good scotch and we stayed up until dawn getting to know each other. We figure we may have played a football game against each other in 1954, we discovered we had Scottish blood and that we were freshly split from our families. He appeared in my column recently as the mysterious McEyebrows (his are two inches long and look like bucktail flies). We had marvellous adventures together, drinking, womanizing, philosophizing. The bartenders along Georgia Street referred to us as the Gold Dust Twins. He taught me to appreciate Burns, Kipling, Service and trout fishing. I taught him to appreciate me the night I held his head over a restaurant toilet bowl as he threw up a rare steak and the remains of a vase of daffodils he had eaten to underscore his complaint that the kitchen was awfully slow bringing his steak to the table. We have travelled all over the province, chasing trout. We make each other laugh. We keep each other sober. The friendship is old now but it just keeps getting better.

In moments when I'm feeling sorry for myself, I often think Lesley is the one great lost love of my life. She gets impatient with that kind of talk because she says our friendship has outlived a lot of love affairs we have both had. I met her in Vernon, where I was playing in a celebrity tennis tournament. She was a hostess, tiny, strawberry blonde, outgoing, intelligent, vivacious. After she moved to Vancouver, at my urging but not to pursue me, I discovered she had a wealth of loyalty, a deep mine of optimism and a driving ambition

to be financially independent. Being a product of my time, this was the first time I had ever had a close relationship with a woman without being obsessed with wedding or bedding her. It was very liberating. She married another guy and moved to Toronto, but as with MacGregor, the friendship endures and ripens.

I had the powerful backing of my five kids, who never gave up on me, who never cease to fascinate me, and who have given me six grandkids. In order, they are Linda, my first-born (the one who served me the Kool-Aid and crackers breakfast that hung-over morning), cool, worldly, a bit cynical, enormously well read, terrific cook, mother of Alexander; Laura, volatile, creatively talented, hard working, more sensitive than she cares to admit, mother of Ashley; Lisa, tiny bundle of bursting energy, works herself thin at business and parenting, the family gossip, mother of Ryan and Shaun; Lenny, the heir to the Boyd billions, athletic, personable, works hard but can't save a dime, is having too much fun to contemplate marriage; Nancy, the tiny, quiet one who sucked her thumb (would tell me it tasted orange), very wise, impresses me with the strength she displays as a single mother to Nick and Dan.

With all this help, I enjoyed the eighties, watching and covering the exciting times. I tried to become more involved in the operation of the paper, getting to know my colleagues in the newsroom, helping the young ones when and where I could. I tried to write better, to take more chances, to move column writing into new areas. Sometimes it worked, sometimes it didn't.

There is a moment in the working day of every journalist, publisher, editor, editorial writer or columnist, when his or her temperature drops. There may be heart flutters.

It is during the morning ritual of opening the mail. It has its rewards; it has its punishments. I have had letters from people thanking me for turning their lives around. I have also received a small box containing nothing but a dried horse turd. I caught the drift, if not the detail.

But from time to time there will be a letter, a thick, weighty one,

the address obviously typed by an expert, the postage office-franked. The letter within will be on the high class of bond seldom used by people who simply want to tell you what a cloth-eared git you are. As it is unfolded, the top of the first page will be revealed. There will be names up there, many, many names. Names of the senior partners of the law firm that sent you the letter, plus, in smaller letters, the twenty-seven junior associates. Off to the right will be typed the quite reasonable advisory, "Without Prejudice." Don't be sucked in by that little diversion. The letter is on your desk because the senior partners, the twenty-seven associates and a bruised client are mad at you. They all want redress and, if possible, some money from your publisher's contingency fund.

You can't write opinion in newspapers without angering someone. Fact is, you can't always write truth in newspapers without people trying to chill you into silence by hollering libel and slander to cover up their own misdeeds.

I've been lucky. I have received half a dozen lawyer's letters but have never had to go to court. I have never cost my publishers anything but the wages of our retainer lawyer. I have had to get down on my belly and crawl in print a couple of times when I was dead wrong, but the person I wronged settled for a printed retraction, usually drafted by a lawyer. I have also been told by our company lawyers to tell the complainant to go wiz up a frozen rope, so weak was his case.

In the early eighties I received a letter from Vancouver lawyer John Laxton, representing International Woodworkers of America union boss Jack Munro. I had written that Munro's normal conversation was so filled with incendiary curses that one or two radio newsrooms had told their beat reporters to quit taping them; it was too difficult editing the tapes to make them fit for airplay. Laxton's letter said I had damaged his client's reputation and they were considering further action. We all had a good laugh at that one and ignored it. Months later I ran into Laxton and Munro and the three of us had a good laugh over it.

In 1982 I described Dr. Norman Spector, the shadowy deputy

minister to then-premier Bill Bennett, as having very close ties to an Ontario political party. I described those ties inaccurately and was required to print a two-paragraph apology. Spector's lawyers got $200 for legal costs.

But the scariest run-in occurred during Clark Davey's first full year as publisher, in 1980. I made the same mistake I would later make with Spector, this time with the well-known Ottawa mandarins, Sylvia and Bernard Ostry. They were career federal civil servants who flourished most noticeably during the Pierre Trudeau reign. You have to be meticulous in describing civil servants, who must appear to be nonpolitical and whose careers can be scuttled by every new government. I wasn't careful. I allied them with the Liberals and that was wrong. Had I used "liberal," with the non-specific lower-case "l," the Ostrys would have had no case against me. But in using the capital "L" I had, in theory, jeopardized their continuing employment. That is to say, an incoming Conservative, reading and believing my piece, might have fired the partisan pair. The Ostrys were angry. They wanted to go to court to clear their names. And they wanted damages in the neighbourhood of $25,000 each.

Davey groaned when I showed him the letter but he backed me up. I remember very clearly (lawyer's letters, like a hangman's appointment, concentrate the mind) that he said, "We're dead in the water on this one. I know the Ostrys; they sue. They'll insist the case be heard in Ottawa, at their convenience. We'll go and we'll fight it, but we'll lose. The only good thing is that you will never, never do this again." We acknowledged the letter and waited. We kept waiting. Finally, both Ostrys were posted to new jobs in Paris. I never heard another word from them and that $50,000 in jeopardy money stayed in the publisher's till.

In 1982, writing on one of my favourite rants — beer commercials on radio and television — I noted that Peter Hyndman, a one-time Social Credit cabinet minister had, before entering politics, been a legal advisor and lobbyist for the B.C. Association of Broadcasters. There was a clear implication of conflict of interest.

The first letter from Hyndman's lawyers came by courier. It charged defamation, demanded an immediate apology for the implied conflict and denied categorically that Hyndman had ever represented the BCAB.

I was pretty sure of my source, but that was all I had. I begged management and our lawyers not to cave in. But I had to have something. I couldn't even find a wooden pop gun, let alone a smoking pistol. Finally, I asked the remarkable Shirley Mooney, the brilliant *Sun* head librarian, to research every BCAB meeting ever held. And somewhere in that labyrinth of files, she found it, on a flimsy yellowed piece of brittle onion paper, the list of counsel appearing before a 1969 licensing commission meeting. Page 122, Appendix 1, eleven names down, listed P.S. Hyndman as "Counsel For British Columbia Association of Broadcasters." Voilà. It had only happened once and so long ago that Hyndman swore he had forgotten it. I was happy to believe him. Case dismissed.

In all those cases, and in my impaired driving charge, I was represented by the flamboyant, theatrical lawyer Peter Butler, who is so much fun, so eccentric, it is almost worth being sued just to spend time with him. Butler bailed Allan Fotheringham out so many times, often with settlements on the courthouse steps, that they became fast friends and Foth became convinced that he and Butler were unbeatable. Dr. Foth was only half right.

In a 1984 *Maclean's Magazine* column, Fotheringham wrote a clumsy sentence that seemed to say that two young Vancouver lawyers, close supporters of John Turner, were involved in a wife-swapping circle. One of the lawyers Fotheringham named had worked with him and with me in the *Sun* sports department when we were all young. The two lawyers, of course, sued immediately. Fotheringham wrote a smart-assed apology in the next edition that did not satisfy the injured parties. Eighteen months later, the case proceeded to court in Vancouver but not until the two Vancouver men pulled a master stroke. They retained Peter, the legendary defender of the Foth. *Maclean's* retained Torontonian Julian Porter, a libel specialist, the husband of book publisher Anna Porter (to

whom Irving Layton once wrote a love poem) and a trial lawyer every bit as theatrical as Butler.

The trial was not to be missed. Fotheringham, at the outset, claimed it was all a misunderstanding, a badly written sentence taken out of context. And he reminded all who asked that he had never lost in court.

Two months before trial date, *Maclean's* and Fotheringham printed a second semi-apology. But it wasn't sincere enough to be accepted. During the trial, Butler asked Fotheringham why he had been so hesitant to make a complete and unequivocal apology. Fotheringham told the court, "Mr. Butler taught me everything I know. He taught me never to make an apology you don't believe in. He acted for me many times and I took his advice. He told me, "Don't be bullied into an apology you don't believe in.""

If you weren't Fotheringham or Porter, the whole thing was great fun. I wrote in a column, "Peter Butler, lumpy, rumpled pants, rusty robes, hair sticking up like soda straws, the bencher's version of the English actor Denholm Elliott; and the sleek, robe-snapping easterner Julian Porter, nicely treading a fine line between James Mason's urbanity and Ontario unctuousness." Butler liked it so much that he sent a copy to his mother in Victoria with a note saying, "I shouldn't sue Denny Boyd. I should sue you for not teaching me to comb my hair or stand up straight."

Butler won in a walk. The court found for the plaintiffs, awarding them $10,000 apiece in damages.

The November 15, 1983 issue of the *Sun* carried a four-paragraph story on an inside page. The headline read, "*Sun* editor, writer, Sue Swangard."

The editor was managing editor Bruce Larsen. The writer was me. The Swangard was Erwin. For once, I was going to be on the other side — the suer, rather than the suee.

By that time, Swangard was the president of the Pacific National Exhibition. His one-man style of rule, his autocracy were red meat just waiting to be butchered. I had good contacts within the PNE and I wrote dozens of columns about its problems.

Somewhere along the line, Swangard forgot the primary rule of survival for journalists: never speak to other journalists. While being interviewed for a *Vancouver Magazine* piece, Swannie's racing tongue tripped over a hurdle.

He referred to *Sun* employees under his managership as "treasonous."

He referred to Larsen as "an asshole."

He called me "that son-of-a-bitch."

It all appeared in print. My first reaction was to laugh and think, "Swannie, I'm glad you've got your health back." But the serious people in the serious suits decided this simply wouldn't do, that Swangard had damaged the reputation of the paper and must be brought to heel. I went along for the ride, not so much for the son-of-a-bitch reference but for a later remark in which said he had saved my life during my drinking days. I couldn't swallow that distortion. Swannie didn't drive me to drink but he certainly gave me a road map.

Besides, I thought, this would be a libel trial like no other, an Olympic Games for the entire Canadian media. I really wanted to hear a distinguished judge intone the words "son-of-a-bitch" and "asshole" for a few days in a panelled courtroom. Some of my colleagues warned me that Swangard had an open-and-shut case based on truth of allegation. We'll never know. Larsen and I both heard that Swangard was genuinely worried he might lose his house if damages were assessed. Both of us settled for a contrite apology from the old bulldozer and ate our revenge lukewarm. It tasted just fine.

I saw Swangard many times after the trial and before his death. I never brought up the lawsuit. I was afraid to. He could still do that to me.

Dealing with sobriety, lawyers and deadlines was occasional work. Dealing with my office neighbour Marjorie Nichols was an everyday challenge.

I don't think I ever won an argument with Marjorie Nichols. I'm

not sure I ever shared what might be called a dialogue with her. I don't like to admit it, but I may never have finished a sentence in her presence before that contradictory bark, that "Nnn-*o*!", would explode out of her throat like the flat splat of a sniper's bullet that catches you between the eyes and drops you where you stand.

Nichols was intimidating. Back in the late sixties, I shared a *Sun* columnists' office with Pat Carney. She was intimidating, too. I'd come into our little office midafternoon and say "Hi, how are you." Carney wouldn't even look up. She'd grate, "I'm writing." I'd shut the hell up and walk around on tiptoes. I wasn't the least bit surprised that Carney became such a formidable MP and senator. But Marjorie Nichols was tougher, meaner, more cantankerous. For two years in the late eighties, before she moved back to Ottawa on the last leg of her outstanding career, we had adjoining offices at the edge of the *Sun* newsroom. The first day she moved into hers, she came into mine and said, "I've just measured our offices. Mine is three inches wider than yours. Do you have a problem with that? If you do, let's settle it right now." That's the competitor she was.

I have never been a morning person. I like to warm up slowly and write in the afternoon. Nichols was full-tilt boogie the moment her eyes snapped open in the morning. I used to walk softly past her office first thing, to look for signs. She'd be reading the editorials and her column, plucking at her hair. That hair-plucking had the significance of a lioness's tail twitching while studying a fat zebra. If Nichols found an editorial opinion she disagreed with or, God forbid, if she found that a word had been changed in her column, she'd pounce and we were all zebra meat. Repeatedly, she'd storm into my office and demand, "Do you know what those bastards have done now?" I never knew. I never even knew what bastards she was talking about — the ones on Parliament Hill, the ones in the B.C. legislature or the ones that ran our paper. The best answer I could ever muster was "Yes, and they won't get away with it."

I don't think Marj approved my route to column writing, out of the sports department directly into a city column, with no time

spent covering a political beat on any level. So she, obsessed with politics, never had much interest in my opinions. The only subject on which she conceded me some authority was alcoholism. She had had her bout with booze and had the scars to prove it. But I could never get over the irony of her sitting in my office chair, directly below my framed copy of the Serenity Prayer, which preaches tolerance, ranting about the stupidity and venality of the population in general.

Strange, though, that when she found out I was diabetic, she was both fascinated and concerned. She volunteered to be my emergency nurse, asking for precise instructions on what she should do "if I come in and find you on the floor drooling and with your eyeballs rolled up." I think part of her wanted to be a nurse to all her male acquaintances. She nagged her best friend, Jack Webster, incessantly about his lifestyle. After she quit drinking, she became convinced that everyone who was still drinking was just one more belt away from an ugly death. She and Webster were such wonderful pals — and it was a friendship based largely on competitive one-upmanship — that I once suggested to Webster that they should become roommates, as Nichols had been with *Globe and Mail* writer Hugh Winsor in their early Ottawa days. Despite their mutual compatibility, Webster reacted as if I had suggested he spar a few rounds with Mike Tyson.

Nichols had a sense of humour, or at least of irony, and a warm smile. But she didn't laugh very often. She was better equipped to disarm with anger or the threat of anger. Her tirades at editors, her smoking memos, were legendary. Few people ever felt entirely secure in her presence. But what she did worked for her. She broke into a male-dominated medium. She proved she could be just as tough, as single-minded, as aggressive as any man that ever stomped across a newsroom. She was a must-read for every politician in Ottawa and the provincial capitals. And every other journalist read her. She didn't just survive in national political writing, she dominated it. When former B.C. premier Dave Barrett cursed her obscenely in the legislative corridor, Nichols cursed him right

126

back and never held a grudge. She was often wrong in her written opinions, but she never apologized, never explained, never backed up a step.

Her work ethic was Herculean. She would no more miss a column than miss a breath. I read once that Arthur Hailey never went a day without writing and that he had once written his daily output, in pencil, while hanging upside down in a traction harness. The last time I spoke to Nichols by telephone, she was in a Vancouver hospital, filled with spreading cancer, having collapsed while attending a Social Credit leadership convention. She was weak, gaunt and they had her hooked up to an overhead IV bottle. She wrote her column in longhand, pushed the entire IV apparatus down the hall to a pay phone and dictated the column down the line to the *Ottawa Citizen*.

Right from the start, she treated her cancer as if it were a nasty political scandal that had to be brought to light and wiped out. It began with a persistent bronchial cough that she attributed to the cold Ottawa winters and the fact that she had "smoked like a peat bog for twenty-five years." But she had a coughing fit that collapsed a lung and Webster, visiting her in Ottawa, took her to hospital (but not before she finished a column). I called her there. She told me they had found a tumour on her lung. A realist, she assumed it would be malignant. But she was typically bitchy: "This is the first time since I was born that I've been in a hospital. I didn't expect the Holiday Inn but, my God! The bed is a slab of concrete with a sheet on it. I'm sore in every bone in my body and the pillows are like lumps of lard covered with plastic. Jack packed my bag when he brought me in and it was typical Jack. I have four toothbrushes and no eyebrow pencils."

When chemotherapy burned her hair off, she bought a huge assortment of turbans and colourful bandanas, forty-two of them, to hide her baldness. When the strain of covering the Hill began to sap her strength, she bombed around on a $900 donut-wheeled mountain bike. After that, she walked with a cane. The cancer spread but she fought it every inch. After two years of it, she told

127

my colleague Vaughn Palmer, "The doctors gave me twenty-six weeks to live at the outset and now that I'm not half-dead, they're paying attention." The message was, don't give up.

She died in hospital in Red Deer. Alberta, December 29, 1991 and I am told she did not go easily. She went out angry. She was forty-eight years old.

Nichols was an enigma. For all her ease in the hallways of power, she was a country girl, born to a family of successful dairy farmers, and she loved rural Alberta. As a girl she was a champion speed-skater. But why did she grow up so angry, so excessively judgemental? There are clues that survived her.

Her *Ottawa Citizen* colleague Paul Gessell wrote a wonderfully warm tribute to her but added intriguingly, "And while friends and family stood beside her in her final agonizing years, it was impossible to avoid the feeling that this was a lonely woman, who was perhaps as insecure as the rest of us despite her pontifications. She was a woman obsessed, carrying the world on her shoulders, Canada's problems were her problems and those problems never ceased to outrage her. The line between politics and her personal life disappeared many years before she died."

She spent much of her last months dictating her memoirs to her friend Jane O'Hara, a first-rate journalist who wrote the posthumous biography *Mark My Words*. There are clues in those pages as well.

In the book Nichols confesses, "To this day, too, my family maintains that I terrorized them with [my] behaviour, controlling them with bad moods and my mean verbalizing. I was a mean little verbalizer. I didn't know that then. Children don't. But I did know that if I was mean enough, I could get my own way."

Her brother Sydney recalled, "She was a wild kid, terrible, absolutely nuts. My parents just couldn't handle her. She and Dad were always at war. Everyone in our family was pretty well scared of her."

After the book's publication, I had a long lunch with O'Hara, who had seen Nichols at her most vulnerable. I told O'Hara, "The

book left me with a bad feeling. Marjorie was not a very nice person."

O'Hara agreed. "I had the same thought, many times. I'd come home from one of our taping sessions and I'd ask myself, 'Why am I doing this. Do I even like Marjorie? She's charismatic, I'm entertained by her but I'm not sure she's a very nice person.' But the more I stayed with her and the more I heard her story, the more I found that my reaction cut both ways, that the adult Marjorie was a product of her childhood. And when I got really deeply into her relationship with her father, I began to think, 'No wonder you're like you are.'"

O'Hara discovered that Nichols was beaten by her father when she was a little girl, starting when she was three and lasting until she left the farm. O'Hara told me, "The other members of the family saw the beatings. Her mother never once interceded and Marjorie never gave in to him. He'd be whipping her and she'd be screaming at him, 'Fuck you, hit me again, I'm as tough as you are.'

"For the rest of her life, Marj remembered those beatings and they shaped her whole personality. She fought with her father every time they met, but she always hoped for his approval. Because her mother had never stepped in and stopped the beatings, Marj wanted no part of being a conventional woman, if it meant being powerless like her mother. Those were the factors that gave Marj the toughness to succeed in the male world of political reporting, the reason she was obsessed with controlling people with her anger or with bribery, the way her father had punished and bribed her to make her cave in to him. She may have been a kid of three when all this started, but she stood up to her father even at that age, so when she grew up, standing up to a prime minister was a piece of cake. And at the end of her life, after all she had lived through, the growing up, the drive to be the best at her job, the drinking, the terrible grape juice and librium hangover mornings, she was still a frightened little girl."

Small wonder that so many of us knew so little about the legend that was Marjorie Nichols.

CHAPTER 11

A couple of times I have had Vancouver television people call and say they want to follow me around, to film the interesting day of a columnist. I've always declined. I don't know what they expected but I'm sure it was something more invigorating than me reading out-of-town papers, me on the phone or reading files or eating soup at my desk. Except for walkabouts, or the occasional interview over lunch (and you can't take notes while you're scarfing down tacos), developing and writing a column is a thinking thing and not very telegenic.

Let me give you an example. In 1989, first thing in the first morning, I decided to keep a daily journal. It was a lucky shot. The year 1989 was the most tumultuous of all the years I could remember at the *Vancouver Sun*. There seemed to be changes or rumours of changes in top and middle management every month. There were format changes, deadline changes and often desperate searches for a *search* for a sense of purpose. At times it seemed the paper was on the verge of ideological collapse. It was the worst of times, with very little sign of relief from the best of times. I wasn't happy at work. I felt I was being undercut and second-guessed by the middle brass. It was terribly upsetting. I was staying sober with the help of my Thursday night twelve-step group. I was trying to stay close to my kids, occasionally resenting their growing up and away.

I wrote it all down.

It is neither typical nor atypical of a year in any large newspaper. It is just an up-close interpretation of one year.

So Happy New Year and away we go.

Jan. 1. Blah day, grey as old socks. At Lautens' house party yesterday, Bill Littler was there from Toronto. Asked me about retirement plans. Told him economics dictate I hang on for another four years. "No problem," he said. "It's only another 1,000 columns." Jeez! . . . depression.

Jan. 3. Back to work. Whoopee. Six years dry today. Glory be and good for me.

Jan. 5. Gordo calls me in to see new column logo. Not bad. Scoop is that Nicole P. will run on A2. He says she'll be the emotional ranter, leaving me to do my thing. So everything goes back to where it was before all the makeovers began. Nick Hills announcement expected shortly. Fear and loathing.

Jan. 6. Haysom says that Hills — he's now official as ed-in-chief — wants A3 for international news. So I may be heading for B1. Why don't I care?

Jan. 7. The Greek tells me Pez and new wife have split. Will follow it up.

Jan. 8. Got to Pez. He confirms it's rocky ("Fuckin' awful") but says lawyers not into it. The Greek, Wally D. and Nick the Banker supply details. Bears are out of NFL playoffs. Shit. Spoke to daughter Linda in Tulsa. She sounded pretty good.

Jan. 9. Wrote the Pez piece despite not being able to track down Mrs. Pez. Should stand up.

Jan. 10. Morning sweat time. MacG. wants comment from Mrs. Pez. Still can't track her. She calls me at 11:30. Carves me a whole new one. Denies everything, calls my column utter trash. I get couple of reaction paras into five-star. There are doubting looks around the newsroom although Gord Fisher loves the piece. Pam Fayerman reads Mrs. Pezim's comments to Pezim. God bless him, he says Susan's version is bullshit. My column is validated. Murray's a strange guy, but he's a standup guy.

Jan. 12. Got a good impression of Nick Hills at introductory reception. Seems approachable, happy to have *Sun* job. Appears to

be a power play at corporate level as to who gets Keate's old corner office.

Jan. 13. Feel on verge of flu or death, whichever comes first.

Jan. 14. Holy sheepshit! Called The Greek to thank him for Pez tip. Now he tells me corespondent will be Tammy the Broker, the bride's best friend and daughter of the pastor who married the Pezims. Bizarro.

Jan. 16. Dinner at Salmon House with Capt. Toot on his forty-fourth birthday. Ran into Bryan Adams at reception desk and he dropped by our table later. He's genuinely passionate about pre-serving heritage houses. An old-fashioned kid, really sincere about his values. He bought our dessert.

Jan. 17. Good to see change in Frank Rutter. He has Marjorie off his back and now The Druid is gone. Having survived a lot of attempts on his job, Frank celebrates by bringing St. Pierre back to pages. I love it.

Jan. 21. To Terminal City Club for retirees' party. Delightful talk with Mr. Hutch. He expressed interest in my recent housing column. Says he's concerned for his five grandchildren. Great to see Hutch and Vaughn together, like father and son.

Jan 25. Nancy fears she may be developing diabetic symptoms: fatigue, thirst. Hope it's just pregnancy complications.

Jan. 28. In a toothache daze for three days. Tylenol got me to sleep but some boozed-up airhead phoned at 4 A.M. to ask where Sean Penn is staying.

Jan. 31. The Dodger is off the wagon. In three days at Whistler and at home, he drank a quart of brandy, four to six (he's not sure) bottles of wine and was down to sipping Grenadine. Christ, is he sick. Christ, does he deserve it. MacEyebrows and I twelve-stepped him at his house. He's all puke and twitch. The problem? He quit going to meetings.

Feb. 3. One of those days that makes it easy to be in the bird cage business. Cute letter from a six-year-old to B.M. the P.M. Talked to his mom, his brother and his teacher and I have a column. God bless Fridays and bright kids. Earlier had written that

the writing on television newscasts is of note-to-the-milkman quality. Tony P. called to order two quarts of homogenized.

Feb. 8. Funny day at work. Apparently, Nick H. is tennis fan. Sensing this, Gord Fisher tore apart sports pages between editions to get in picture and two stories on Bjorn Borg. Good thing, in long run. One of the stories that was dropped referred to Karen Percy not being able to ski because of 'depilitating' case of flu. (Yep, that can really chafe, especially in the downhill.) It's up there with recent story of Bank of Hong Kong lobby clock with pendulum that "swang." (Like a pendulum do?)

Feb. 9. Jack Webster in to see Nick. Denies it, but obviously looking for a job, a column. He's bored without an audience. Coincidentally, McRanor asked me how long it would take me to read my column aloud. Suspect he's trying to relate print space to air time for Jack's benefit. Jack told me at VPD police band dinner that something was offered — maybe my space on my day off — but he said the money was "insulting."

Feb. 12. Hal Straight died today. John Armstrong called from newsroom to tell me. Nice kid, he thought I'd want to know right away.

Feb. 13. Hadn't planned to write anything about Straight but Alex MacG. pushed and I listened and I'm glad I did. It's a pretty good column but more than that, it's a proper record of why the things guys like him did thirty to forty years ago are important to the new generation. Alex has good judgement, must always remember that.

Feb. 14. Lavishly warm memo from Hills re: my abortion column. Handwritten in Keate style. Jamie has great idea. Wear white shirts, keep memo in breast pocket so the colour shows. Walk past M.E.'s office all week. He'll go ape wondering what memo says. Palmer tells me Nicole to get an extra column each week: "Letters to Nicole." Is that how Ann Landers got her start?

Feb. 18. Home again after 3½ days in hospital. Blood sugars totally fucked up. Apparently backlash of the abscessed tooth caused the problem.

Feb. 19. I'll be damned. Dr. Tom Perry, who handled my heart

attack in 1980, beat den Hertog and got the NDP nomination for Van Pt.Grey by-election. He could win the seat.

Feb. 20. My dentist tells me the hospital stay was caused by yeast infection in mouth. Something called candida. Sounds like nineteenth-century novel. Talk to Tom Perry. Tell him he can win if he avoids traditional socialist rant.

Feb. 21. More talk about page 3 redesign. Better pack a bag. Looks like I'm on the move again.

Feb. 22. All the brass — Hills, Fisher, Rutter, Macrae — over to Victoria because Hills wanted to meet Hutchison and Victoria bureau. Couldn't send him over there without a convoy, could we?

Feb. 23. Spent morning on Powell Street, looking for signs of new life suggested by civic report. No such signs but talked to some nice people and had great lunch in all-you-can-eat Japanese sushi deli, a real find.

Feb. 24 Spoke to medical chiefs-of-staff of all B.C. hospitals. Went okay. They laughed in the right places.

Mar. 2 Jamie's back from Ottawa and Meech talks. He's really depressed over his worsening situation in the paper. They just cannot seem to slot him and give him a mandate, a vote of confidence. It's ridiculous. He works hard, has a good attitude and always produces a good read. Seems somebody has sold him out.

Mar. 4. Ed Broadbent quit and I made a great pot of meatball soup. One of us had a good day.

Mar. 5. Have been offered trip to USSR. Will smell it out. If arrangements aren't guaranteed 100 per cent foolproof, to hell with it.

Mar. 7. Talk to G.F. about Soviet trip. He says we never know when Aeroflot flights crash unless they hit hard enough to trigger western seismograph trackers. Thanks for sharing that, Gord.

Mar. 9. Lunch with Bryan Adams at Hilde's Tea Shop. Then, on hunch, to Pan Pacific to hear Harcourt drop bombshell on elite group of big business types. Says he wants to be friends with business, surely a radical shift and one that will win him some soft sup-

port. More and more, it looks like Vander Zalm and Socreds are dead as vaudeville.

Mar. 10. Supreme Court of Canada kicked abortion definition back to federal government today and much shit hits many fans. Civil-righter Joe Boroski accuses judges of being drunk, says he wishes he could punch them all out. Looks as if blockades, civil disobedience and court proceedings are just beginning. And the Soviet trip is on.

Mar. 13. Snarly, gnarly. Down several quarts of essential juices.

Mar. 15. Big victory for Tom Perry in Pt. Grey by-election, took more votes than Levy and Wilson combined. NDP also won in Nanaimo. Socreds reeling. Vander Zalm looked pale on television. There's speculation he'll step down but I doubt it. More likely he'll call snap election in fall. Pull it together or go down in flames and let someone else rebuild the party,

Mar. 16. Breakfast with Tony and Fred L. at Bay of Pigs. Lots of laughs. Tony has new five-year contract which will take him to fifty-five. Both seem happy with their marriages. As we leave, Tony goes to his silver Jag, Fred to the Caddie he got after the Porsche, me to my Omni. To work, for one of those days when writing is like putting one brick on another brick.

Mar. 17. Funny chat with Alex about G.F.'s talent for disparaging everything we were doing with the paper in the sixties. But the paper looks and reads well. G.F. is a very creative editor, just that his judgements on people are volatile and inconsistent. Ian H. says my current popularity with the brass is a matter of being "the flavour of the month."

Mar. 22. Another boy for Nancy and Tito, a fourth grandson for me. Daniel Jason Alphonso Campos is a beautiful baby, exquisitely shaped head, tiny red fingers, blue eyes. Laura is entranced with him, threatens to steal him. Amazing how maternal my daughters are. Lunch with Lenny at Beijing. Hellacious feed for only $21.

Mar. 25. Great going-away party for sports ed. Dunc Stewart. Archie and Jack Lee did terrific job arranging it. Best line from

Pogo L., talking about old sports department days "when Jack Lee was a minority."

Mar. 26. Happy Easter. No eggs for this boy.

March 31. Took Len to Pezim roast. Meal okay but nine hundred people had their ears and intelligence insulted by grunge jokes from the cream of Las Vegas comics, the worst being Joan Rivers.

Apr. 5. Jamie and I have been asked to give up our offices and move into executive flanking Nick H. Or, we can have PCs put into our homes. Seems there's a shortage of space. I'll rely on Jamie's judgement. He always knows what's happening.

Apr. 6. Lots of good newspapering done today; wish I'd done some of it. Breaking stories on deadline; huge make-overs; Ken West filling in as news editor; everyone pulling weight. Emrick absolutely ecstatic. I enjoy the way he enjoys doing his job. But Haysom whispers that *Province* editor-in-chief job is his. Damn. If I were ten years younger, I'd go with him.

Apr. 7. A minor hostage-taking on Parliament Hill today, using a Greyhound bus. How wonderfully Canadian. Nothing on the wires, Ottawa paralyzed. But Larry Emrick phoned Southam News office, got them to give him an eyeball description. Brilliant. We chased four-star for line story. We probably beat every paper outside of Ontario. Should be bonuses for that kind of enterprise.

Apr. 8. Watched grandson Shaun play soccer today. The little bugger can play. Good moves, very heady, scored a lovely goal. Then to Vancouver College to speak at fund-raiser in honour of Archbishop Carney. Sat with His Grace, found out he has terrific sense of humour.

Apr. 9. Made fifty pot-stickers from scratch. Lenny came over to pick up a plateful, with his Flavour of the Weekend, a divorcee.

Apr. 12. Sagi miffed today. He was reading a job-posting on the bulletin board, for general features writer, when he realized it was his job. No one had told him. Every day, it seems, page one is filled with stories I don't understand, don't give a damn about and can't get columns from. Is it me or should decision-makers lighten up. This is *Vancouver Sun*, not *Times* of London.

136

Apr. 17. Hard to believe it but there it is. Thin Monday paper and heavy weekend of news — Brit soccer deaths, Exxon oil mess, new charges against Bennett Brothers, federal Libs battered again, Turner rumoured to be stepping down. But we run ten pages, plus humungous page one picture, on the 10-k Sun Run, including six pages of six-point results, listed alphabetically. In the history of the paper, I doubt that we have given ten pages to any news story. What an orgy of self-congratulation.

Apr. 19. Jamie says at lunch that board was knocked out by Haysom's pitch for *Province* job. Apparently all current *Province* editors have been ruled out. That's no surprise.

Apr. 21. A call from Soviet embassy in Ottawa. Igor wants to be my "breedge" for USSR trip.

Apr. 22. Moderated panel at Alcohol-Drug Education Services meeting. We drew maybe sixty people to talk about high-risk juvenile drug users. Meanwhile, they got thirty-thousand out for the annual feel-good peace march.

Apr. 24. Funny story about Nick at lunch today. When he was leaving Southam news, he let it be known that he wanted some antique furniture as a going-away gift. Instead they gave him a tailor-made Napoleon-type cocked hat. He was livid. So was Southam when they got $18,000 bill for the party, which had a five-hour open bar.

Apr. 25. Was heading out for library board meeting when bulletin came out that Global News had leaked Wilson's federal budget. Home at 9 for call from Ken West. They are loading A3 with budget news, making my column irrelevant. I suggested they dump my column, use my space. Felt shitty immediately. Said I'd come in, do new piece. Newsroom like V-E Day operations centre, everyone working. My piece was all over the map but was appropriate. Home at 1 A.M., bloated with pizza, sleepless with coffee but bloody exhilarated. This is the fun of newspapering.

Apr. 27. Still cracked up over best budget story. They sent John Armstrong out to get man-on-street reaction. He asked one old dear what she thought of the budget. "Budgies?" she said, "Never did like budgies." Monty Python lives.

May 3. John Turner resigned as Liberal leader and we made a meal of it. Terrific coverage in the home edition.

May 7. Had a long telephone chat with Haysom. He's got the *Province* job. I'll miss him and if I didn't have Nick H. on my side, I'd jump with him. He was a damned good friend when I was having problems with G.F. Ian thinks he landed the job with the line in his presentation that said, "This paper was designed by a promotions manager. It's time to let a journalist take a crack at it." It will be interesting to see if he can shape up the *Province*'s stable of dozing, dilettante columnists. He says he plans to.

May 9. Met Tony P. for coffee. Goddamn him he looks camera-ready at any time of day, no matter what he's wearing. But the column I got proves how hard it is to interview your friends. It was lousy.

May 11. Apologized to Andy for cutting up on him at last meeting. He wiggled his eyebrows at me and I felt better . . . He and Joan are off on three-week trip down coast on their Harleys.

May 13. Nancy phoned. Tito has walked out. I gave her a lawyer's name and told her to change the locks. Christ, what a record this family has, eight divorces and Lenny isn't married yet.

May 14. Talked to couple of *Province* guys in cafeteria, assured them that Haysom's a nice guy and a good journalist. Lots of apprehension over there. Good. Might wake up some of those lazy, smug bastards from the sleep they've been in the past ten years.

May 15. Jamie's situation deteriorating. They're discontinuing his column, advising him to apply for op-ed spot that might come open. He's been wracking his brain, trying to figure why this has come down on him, who he has crossed.

May 16. Webster in my office today, all nerves and bluster. They've offered him a once-a-week column, even though no one knows if he can write. Jack admits he has his doubts. What the hell are we doing? Management is scuttling a talented forty year old and recruiting a seventy year old. Christ!

May 18. Suddenly there's Soviet action coming out of the yin-yang, after weeks of inaction. Novosti Press, my host, is suggesting

four-city tour: Moscow, Kiev, Odessa and a fourth to be named later, possibly in Siberia. They say two weeks, Gord says has to be three, four, to do it right. I'm for three. Not admitting it, but this is the assignment of a lifetime.

May 23. Front page box announces addition of Geoffrey Stevens to *Sun*'s "stable of columnists." Stable! Jamie and I have a vaudeville routine. "How many columnists are there in the *Sun* stable?" Then we stomp one hoof eighteen times. Webster occupying Haysom's office. One day on the job and he gets an office with a window.

May 25. Fisher has assigned Shelley Fralic as my editor on the USSR project. Except that I can't take her with me, that's great. I like her judgement and story ideas and she'll be a good Momma to talk to when I'm over there. And Webster has jammed out. They gave him an office, a secretary, his own editor, a big money offer and a month to produce his first weekly column. He told them yesterday that he can't handle it. On radio or TV, winging it, he's the best in Canada. But he went to pieces at the prospect of writing once a week. Hope this leaves him with more respect for those of us who do five a week.

May 26. Gordo wants me to do the line story on demolition of Georgia Medical Centre this weekend. Write the hell out of it, he said. With instructions like that, how could a guy go wrong?

May 28. Up at 4 A.M., in town at 5 for 5:45 blast. Blast was delayed but when it went, it went perfectly, dropping the building like a bun from a tall cow's bum. Home for quick nap, into office to write pretty fair thirty-incher.

Jun. 2. Nightmare last night. I was on trial in Moscow, Brezhnev was the judge, prosecutor and defence counsel. Wouldn't tell me what I was charged with, only that it was serious. When I said I couldn't hear him he poured warm oil in my ears and swabbed them with Q-tips. Weird, but so vivid that there I was at 4 A.M., on the edge of the bed, afraid to go back to sleep.

Jun. 4. World is going mad. Death toll in Beijing, 1,400. Deng's army has been burning bodies, making count suspect. Khomeini

dead in Iran, mourners are climbing his balcony to kiss his chair. In Russia, a pipeline exploded as two trains were passing, eight hundred dead, many of them kids on way to summer camps.

Jun. 7. Boring day. Shopped. Bought a Batman T-shirt. Someone stop me before I shop again.

Jun. 8. Mom phoned from Victoria, wanted to assure me that the house is still there. Thought she was laying a guilt trip on me for not visiting. But someone planted a bomb in a car two doors away and her front yard was covered with car debris. Looks like amateur hit. You don't plant bomb in front of engine block if you know what you're doing.

Jun. 10. Laura called, wants to get whole family together for birthday — Father's Day barbecue. Good idea, if there's anything good about turning fifty-nine.

Jun. 13. Ran into Jim Coleman. Haysom has hired him to do background pieces on major sports events. Kidded him about finally finding work. The guy is seventy-five, still sharp, still a witty writer with a million stories to tell. Wish I felt the same. I can't tell if I'm ill, down a quart or just sick and tired of work. Wish I could afford to retire.

Jun. 15. Barbecue bash with kids and grandkids. Lots of laughs, moose steaks and they gave me a gorgeous gold medical alert medallion. Later, a phone call from Igor at Soviet embassy. Word is I depart Mirabel for Moscow Aug. 6, do Moscow, Kiev, Odessa and Yakutsk. Depart Moscow Aug. 20. And please send $50 for visa.

Jun. 18. Turned fifty-nine. It was more fun than a rat-killing. Mom, Nancy, Lisa and Greg phoned. Watched U.S. Open. Had pie for dessert. Had a bath. Bet sixty will be a real pisser.

Jun. 25. I was so ticked off at having to go in today that I was hoping to run into Nick. Wanted to say, "I'm the oldest columnist west of Trent Frayne and not only am I still doing five a week but you've got me coming in Sundays. Aren't you ashamed?" But Nick doesn't come in Sundays so I shut the hell up and wrote my column.

Jul. 2. Tried to phone Lesley in Toronto but she's not in. Just as

well, I'd have said something stupid. Maybe it's healthy to be half-assed in love with someone you never see and seldom talk to. The perceptions remain perfect.

Jul. 4. Most peculiar thing in paper today. We had the phrase "cock-teaser" in a book review. Every reporter saw it in first edition and talked about it. But it ran all editions untouched because, apparently, no editor saw it. Had dinner with Mike Cramond. He and Thelma married fifty years. He gave me some trout flies and lesson in line retrieval. While stripping line he made the reel sing. He said, "God I love that sound. That and organ music are all I want at my funeral."

Jul. 10. Got fax from Moscow, detailing three-week trip. Nick says he'll give me the name of favourite vodka he wants me to bring back. Dream on, Nick. Taking a week off to go fishing.

Jul. 13. Got up to Tahwheel Lake up on plateau near Little Fort, just in time to see RCMP dive team bringing in bodies from float-plane crash. Two dead, one survivor, a kid who popped out of the water and climbed up on tail, despite two broken shoulders. Plane's tail sticking out of water like a funeral cross. Collected data, tried to call in story by radio-phone. No success, too much static. Maddening frustration and smell of death takes edge off fishing.

Jul. 17. Left lake, everyone snarling at everyone. Glad this God-cursed trip is over,

Jul. 19. They ran my fishing trip piece on page one. G.F. sent congratulations and message to watch page one in four-star. Later Nick dropped by to say it was his idea. Whatever . . .

Jul. 21. Called Nicole tonight. Lorne has had a stroke. Hope she has strength to pull him through. Figure she has.

Jul. 22. Dinner with Arch at Cafe Roma. Pasta, Italian sausage, much good talk about the paper, colleagues, hope for new regime, good-old and bad-old days, our long past and shortening future and our kids. And he picked up the tab.

Jul. 24. Now it's Moira, the best reporter on the paper, who's pissed off and wants me to call Haysom at *Province* to say she's ready to jump. She's off to Winnipeg to cover massive forest fires.

She says, "Covering a little fire isn't going to keep me happy for the next ten years." Now that's mad.

Jul. 25. Doctor says I have a broken rib. Did it on fishing trip. Tells me to expect six to eight weeks of mild pain. Going to be a bitch packing luggage around USSR.

Jul. 27. Soviet planning meeting. Nick doesn't want me to write until I get back. Has some Cold War surveillance jitters. Gord says that's too long with column vacant. I agree. I want to take portable typewriter, file by fax where available.

Jul. 29. Last haircut before Moscow. Jimmy G. told me story about Alaska guy who hooked monster salmon, possibly in hundred-pound range, in fourteen-foot boat. Played it thirty-six hours. His son knocked it off trying to net it. Terrific piece in paper by Susan Balcolm about women living single life. Dead honest. It's a privilege to work with talent like that.

Aug. 1. Shits were trumps when Fralic realized no one has requested visa. Trip could be up a creek just north of Kiev. Much running about ensued. Good old Igor in Ottawa swears he'll fast-track and it will be waiting for me in Montreal. And Yakutsk is out; Yalta and Riga are in. Back to the reference books.

Aug. 4. Got my camera and ten rolls of film. Got my money belt, got my American Express cheques, got triple insulin supply, got spread all over top of page one. Let's do it.

Aug. 5. With a nervous stomach but an heroic attitude, I'm outa here. To be continued.

Chapter 12

In August of 1989, I put aside the heavy green accountant's ledger book that was serving as my chronicle of that year, stuffed a much smaller black notebook in my back pocket and, packing far too much luggage and far too little practical knowledge, flew to the Soviet Union for a three-and-a-half-week walkabout. I had a portable typewriter, a tape recorder I never used (translation problems made it impracticable), traveller's cheques, guide books, pencils, pens, news clippings, consumer items said to be in shortage over there (bathtub plugs, pantyhose, razor blades), five cartons of cigarettes and, mindful of the 1941 newsreel images of German infantrymen freezing to death while standing upright, far too much cold-weather clothing.

The little black notebook was about the only smart travelling decision I made. It became a diary within a diary, the little brother of the larger journal I left behind. Every night, after I had transcribed the notes of the day's formal interviews, I recorded the day's minutiae, all the irritations and experiences of a bad traveller in a bad traveller's destination. Since nothing works in socialist nations, I was in a constantly liverish mood. The little diary became my scratch-pole, preventing me from clawing the furniture or howling at the moon.

Airborne: It's clear that my problem with flying has more to do with airports than airplanes. After a $50 cab ride from downtown Montreal to Mirabel airport, I was in a stomach-churning, oozing-

nervous sweat, imagining all manner of problems, thinking of a dozen reasons I should have turned the assignment down. But as soon as we boarded — and I think I'm the only non-Soviet on the flight — everything settled down. Flight crew amiable, stewies husky. Take-off and emergency procedures not announced but printed on cards in four languages, but not English. All the lavatory soap gone, stolen, forty-five minutes into flight. One-hour pitstop in Gander, free Pepsi for everyone, heavy on the duty-free booze counter. Hot roast beef dinner served at midnight my time. Six hours to Moscow.

Moscow, first day. Didn't take long to see the Soviet system at work — at dead idle. De-planed at Sheremetyevo Airport, passed visa and passport checks, filled in customs declaration, claimed luggage, met problem. Customs requires sworn declaration that incoming passenger is not bringing any Soviet currency into country. Prison term threatened for violations. No problem. I signed. Grabbed rusty luggage cart. Young guy in charge of them demands five kopeks. How could I have five kopeks in my pocket. It's against the law. I look around. Every other deplaning passenger is buying a luggage cart with kopeks. Will they be seized, dragged off to filthy prisons? No, the militia men in the room look on, bored, at all these acts of perjury. I'm the only honest person in the vast room. I'm also the only one without a luggage cart. In mime and broken English, I managed to beg five kopeks from amused Russian passengers. Then I get a luggage cart. I wheel into line for customs check.

Two-and-a-half hours later I have moved ten feet. Only one customs line is open; four others are closed. From my shoulder bag, I pull out a *Vancouver Sun* baseball cap. Minutes later, I see a young man and a security guard heading my way. Are yellow hats against the law, too? No, the young man is my host, my guide, my translator and will become my friend. He is Serge V. Tsyganov of Novosti Press's Canada-U.S. News Desk, twenty-five years old, a bachelor, speaks almost perfect English. His business card says "Editor and Stuff Writer." Oh well.

144

He had been waiting outside with a car for two hours, grew concerned, talked his way through security and hauled the security man in with him. Spotted my cap. "Let's get out of here," he says. "I haven't cleared customs," I say. "Not to worry," he says, "You have blat." There were two hundred morose Russians in front of me in the line. We bypass them all, are out of there in thirty seconds, luggage unexamined.

In the car I ask Serge, "How did you do that? What's this blat?" He smiles. "Special privilege," he says.

On the drive in, we pass a huge, rough sculpture, seemingly made from chunks of railroad track. It's an artistic rendering of a tank trap and it marks the deepest penetration of the German infantry in 1941. There they were stopped; there the counter-attack began; there the end of the Second War began. It's a bit breathtaking.

My hotel is the Sovietskaya, rated "above A" in guide books. Quite nice. Stalin-era, huge lobby, curving marble double staircase. Snarly old bell captain who doesn't carry luggage. Gorgeous redhead concierge takes my visa and passport, stores them in vault. I shower, go for walk, see first food lines, for bruised peaches, hard green tomatoes. I get concierge — I've nicknamed her Ravishin' Ruby, from a Tom T. Hall song — to make a dining room reservation. But when I go in later on, miserable bastard at the desk has no reservation, no English, no manners, no interest in seating me even though every table is empty. No blat here. I fetch Ravishin' Ruby, she gives him screaming hell, I get seated. Eat, go to bed.

Moscow, second day: Serge and I go to the Arbat, equivalent to Vancouver's Fourth Avenue in 1960s — hippies, poets, musicians, public haranguers. Then to Red Square, the Kremlin walls, magnificent St. Basil's Cathedral, GUM department store (the size of the legislative buildings in any Canadian prairie capital), Lenin's tomb and Loby Square, with the stone block where the czars had their enemies' heads chopped off. When I tell Serge how the very name, the Kremlin, used to make us nervous during the Cold War, he says, "We have killed all our monsters." Serge is not sold on

Gorbachev, is impressed with Kohl, politely noncommittal about Mulroney.

My shower curtain is driving me crazy. It's made of fine linen mesh, eighteen inches wide, eight feet long and hangs on a moveable rod near the shower head. No matter how I stretch it, I still get water on the marble floor. It's beginning to irritate me.

Third day: My room service breakfast was interesting. I asked for two eggs, toast, big pot of coffee. What was wheeled in was an omelet, six fried eggs, a platter of cheese, a platter of cold cuts, two half-loaves of bread, a carafe of hot water but no coffee. I was halfway through the omelet when the poor waiter came back. "Eez mistake," he says. I help him load the stuff back on his car, swipe a pot of coffee. Seems to fit the expression Serge has taught me, "Eta Zsheezen." It's life.

We drove past the Danilov Monastery, thirteenth-century Russian Orthodox. When Reagan was coming here, his advance people asked to have the Danilov approach road paved for his limo. Metropolitan Filaret, the high clergyman said, "One does not ride to see God; one walks on one's feet or one's knees." Reagan walked.

Moscow is a fascinating city but too decrepit to be a great one. It needs paint, it needs building repairs, it needs Weed-Wackers to trim the grass in the parks and along the eight-lane roads. It looks tired and who wouldn't be, packing that load of history. So many of the buildings have needle-like spires, it's clear why Hitler didn't send in the paratroops; they'd have been skewered.

We drove out to the 550-metre-high television tower. It is tightly secured against terrorist attacks. Elevators go up like stink. A few seconds of stomach dropping and we're at 330-metre level, a revolving restaurant with a breathtaking view of Moscow, the city that was founded as a wooden fort on the banks of the Volga in 1147 by Prince Yuri Dolgoruky (Yuri the Long-Armed). Yuri didn't mow the lawns and neither has anyone else. We have a decent lunch and Serge buys a bottle of Scotch for his father, who is in the foreign ministry.

We stop off at the offices of the editor of a newsmagazine,

Arguments & Facts, with a weekly circulation of 22 million. The editor has mixed emotions about Gorbachev, thinks he's too showy. He says Yeltsin has no chance of assuming leadership if Gorbachev fails. Puts it in a nice perspective for me. "Everyone likes him but no one will vote for him. Like your Edward Broadbent." He is absolutely fascinated by Canadian agricultural efficiency ("the best in the world") and clearly bored by my questions about abortions in USSR. Can't understand why Canada is debating it. On the way back to the hotel we stopped, at my request, at a butcher store. Rank smell, lots of eggs, total meat supply is a lot of leg bones that we would use for soup or toss to the dog. To buy a small piece of white cheese, I deal with three clerks, one to take order, one to wrap it, one to take my money. Soviet constitution guarantees job for every citizen. That's how they do it, through make-work.

Fourth day:I have had two refrigerators, am on a third, and none of them work, though they look new. Amiable repairman and his helper keep coming in, looking, hauling away. Finally, I read something that answers my questions. Mass refrigeration is only fifteen years old in the USSR. That's why so much of their meat spoils during shipping. That's why, after hours of clanking, my fridges produced tiny ice cubes the size of Chiclets. They were working, as best they could. And Serge solves my shower curtain mystery. It isn't my shower curtain, it's my hand towel. Shower curtains in Moscow are like ice cubes. There aren't any.

Serge is a delight. I have warned him that before I leave, I am going to teach him to be laid back. Today, inside the Kremlin, the air suddenly cooled pleasantly. Serge said, "Denny, the hot is receding." He was embarrassed when I cracked up. He's bright, aggressive, conscientious, speaks four languages and earns 200 rubles a month. But he cracks up whenever we come back to my hotel and I say to that surly doorman-porter, "Hello you miserable fart, how are you?" Him I have nicknamed Ivan Pisdov. If he speaks any English, he doesn't admit to it. His entire job seems to be scowling at people, and he does it well.

Saw a funny sight outside the hotel today. A guy walked past

carrying a string shopping bag. It split and a bottle of Teacher's Highland Cream fell out on the sidewalk. It bounced, rolled but didn't break. The guy looked up at the sky and mumbled something. The State frowns on religious worship, but this guy cheated.

Fifth day: We did another walkabout inside the Kremlin walls. One of the tourist musts is the world's biggest cannon, with balls to match. Military built the monster but never fired it, afraid a misfire would kill the gun crew and every villager for a hundred miles around. To repeat, nothing works in the Soviet Union. I stepped off the curb to take a picture and a very snotty militia-man yelled at me to get back on the sidewalk. I was standing in a driving lane reserved for the Kremlin elite, which is a nyet-nyet. I pointed to the stack of balls and then at him but I think he missed my message.

We came back by Metro, the Moscow subway, a super experience. Built by Stalin, it features stunning mosaics, marble from every region in the USSR, and there isn't a gum wrapper, a cigarette butt or a drunk or a panhandler to be seen. It's clean, fast, cheap and there is no graffiti.

The rest of the day was bad. Our afternoon driver bugged off and left us on our own. I had a bowl of terrific soup for lunch but the search for dinner got desperate. We went from one hotel dining room to another. None would let us in. I think we got turned down in all four of Serge's official languages. If you aren't registered or in a tour group, they don't want you. And there are no pizza joints, burger shops or public restaurants. I was beginning to get a hypoglycemic reaction, feeling weak, dizzy. My snack food had gone with our missing driver. I had explained my diabetes to Serge on the first day and he was getting worried. Finally, he talked us into a co-op coffee house. They brought us a platter of meat and cheese and I wolfed it down. Instant recovery. We were seated with two friendly Russians, a journalist and a young agriculture specialist. Both spoke good English. Both were pounding down cherry brandies and wanted me to join them. The journalist was especially drunk; his wife had just left him. When we left I told him I hoped

he would not drink too much because I liked him. He got up and gave me a rib-cracking hug.

Sixth day: Hell of a thunderstorm. When it rains in Moscow, traffic halts. Windshield wipers are "a deficit product" so drivers keep them locked away in their glove compartments to avoid theft. When rain starts, drivers stop where they are, attach wipers, drive on, reversing procedure when rain stops.

I have asked Serge why he and his people yell at each other so much. The simplest negotiation to get into a public building is accompanied by such an harangue I expect fists to fly. Then they stop, say "Spacebo" (thank you) and carry on. Serge says, "We are not angry. It is just the way we talk and it is part of our old village heritage. We want to talk so forcibly that it will astound the other person and they will give us more than they want to. Sometimes we go home and the water faucets aren't working right and we yell, 'Oh you bastards.' But then we remember we are at home with people we love and we don't have to shout."

It made me think about the attitudes of people here in the service industries, surly, resentful, unwilling. But I think the system makes them that way. Rule #1: Nothing works here. Rule #2: Someone must be blamed. Rule #3: Don't be that person; don't volunteer; don't try.

Another thing I have learned. My first few days here, I wondered why everyone looked so grim, why no one smiled. After five days I know. Their life is unrelentingly grim. They have nothing to smile about.

Odessa, day one: Here we are at the Black Sea and guess what? It isn't black. Exclusive news story to follow.

Odd thing happened at Moscow airport. We were walking along tarmac when I heard a voice behind me say, "*Vancouver Sun*? What are you doing here?" The woman was the wife of Christopher Young, the Southam Moscow correspondent. She has just dropped him off, seen my hat, wanted to know what in hell I was doing on her husband's turf. I explained, but she was clearly miffed that no one from Southam had alerted Chris.

149

At Odessa airport, the usual scramble for a taxi. Serge, the idealist, hates to bribe, says it only serves to corrupt everyone.

In Moscow there are 48,000 taxicabs but you don't get one unless you as bribe with a package of Marlboroughs or agree to pay twice or triple the metered fare.

Finally, after thirty minutes of bickering, Serge agreed on triple fare and we got to our hotel thirty minutes after the dining room closed. All we had been given on the flight was a small clay cup of watery mineral water. Famished, hotel unimpressed. So Serge phoned his boss in Moscow. Boss phoned the local Party chief who called the hotel. Result, I sat under a fifteen-foot-high sculpted ceiling in my room surrounded by Louis XV (or knockoff) furniture, being served cold quail and marinated tomatoes by a tuxedoed waiter. Blat, ya gotta love it.

Odessa has been Vancouver's sister city since end of Second World War when a group of Vancouver Jews with Russian roots put together a big shipment of food, blankets and medical supplies for the Odessa people, who had been horribly mistreated by German armies.

We did what must be done on an Odessa visit: we walked down the Odessa steps, fifteen steep ranks of them made famous by the falling baby-buggy scene in the Russian revolutionary film, *Battleship Potemkin*. Fortunately, there is an elevator to get back up. Odessa is a striking-looking seaport city, with beaches, cobbled streets that the old women sweep every morning with home-made brooms, squat buildings with wrought-iron balconies.

I spent a morning visiting and having tea with the mayor, who is aware of the sistership with Vancouver. She assures me that Odessans are still grateful. Odessa taxi drivers share no such emotion. They are just as surly and gouging as their nasty brothers in Moscow.

(Here the journal becomes somewhat disorganized. Weariness, stress, were taking their toll and would continue to do so.)

I believe it is Wednesday. I haven't been totally sure what day it is since I got to this country because it doesn't matter. My time isn't mine; my schedule is set for me and doesn't deviate.

We are in Kiev. It has been totally rebuilt since the Nazis destroyed it. My trip is now half over and I have discovered some surprising things.

Gorbachev's popularity is all in the West. The people I have been talking to, intellectuals, cab drivers, journalists, think he spends too much time cavorting in Bonn and Washington while things are going to hell at home. It may be perestroika and glasnost, but it's still the same old story: line up for hours for a few potatoes or a bar of soap. There are no shoes, no toothpaste, no diapers, no meat, no razor blades, no fruit, no coffee. The official line is that there are no shortages, only deficit products. Make a show of complaining and the mean militia guys move in. And the war news from Afghanistan is bad. But the Soviets see Gorbachev waving his hat, being hailed and paraded in the West as the new saviour of the Soviets, and it disgusts them. One of our drivers growls, "Why is he visiting Washington? Why isn't he here helping me to put a piece of meat on my table?"

The KGB has a public relations department headed by a retired general. All the Moscow reporters have his home number.

The younger Soviets regard the Communist Party as being hopelessly conservative. The circulations of the new liberal newspapers are soaring; those of the official Party papers are declining.

I have yet to see a telephone book in any Soviet city. Serge says he has never seen one either.

Soviet soap smells like bubble gum and it lathers just as well.

The trouble with Soviet toilet paper is quite obvious. They don't remove the bark before the pulping process.

There is a numbing sameness in all the formal interviews I have had with bureaucrats. I am taken into a panelled room, seated at a small table with dusty bottles of Pepsi and orange Fanta. I am seated below a raised dais where they sit like a court-martial jury. There are usually five of them, four in casual clothes, one in a suit. The suit is the boss, who controls the others. Translation goes slowly. I try to break the ice with some humour at the start. Waste of time; they don't do humour.

I met with a health ministry group looking for solutions to alcohol problems. They don't believe in Alcoholics Anonymous, believing it to be church oriented. They want state orientation. The suit tells me alcoholism is not chronic and that they are near several possible solutions, using herbs, hypnosis and a medicine based on a coal extract. At the end of their bench, a husky guy in a golf shirt smothers a grin and rolls his eyes at all this B.S. I meet him outside and he tells me he's an ex-drunk who dried out using what he had heard of AA. We share a good laugh over the coal-tar solution.

A lot of things caught up with me in Kiev, the weary dismals and the dislocation blues. I had an anxiety attack at lunch. I thought I would have to bolt from the table. It was the muggy heat today, the full moon last night. It was not having a clean shirt. It was another mass interview. It was being here almost two weeks and my office hasn't phoned or wired to tell me what a trooper I am, what a great job I'm doing. I need a hug. The Soviet Union doesn't hug, it just squeezes.

Serge snaps me out of it by telling me about some realities. He tells me about gun meat. That's the kind of disposable people the old Soviet regimes have always wanted — gun meat. People who bow down to authority without question, march to any old war, give up their lives without a whimper.

He gets heated as he tell me that his generation will not take it any more. He tells me that he will probably never own a car; only eleven per cent of Soviets own one. He says, "We all live on small credit. We borrow five rubles here, five rubles there just to get by. Even the bosses have to borrow." A married man with a new baby wants good soap to wash his child. To get it, he has to stand in line for hours. It debases him but he has to do it for his baby. He has bad shoes, an old overcoat. He can't afford replacements. He has no luxuries, he doesn't even have necessities. There are 2.7 million marriages a year in the USSR and 900,000 divorces. Serge has a Moscow girl friend but may be doomed to live at home with his parents. He makes two hundred rubles a month. A fifty-square-metre co-op apartment would cost him ten thousand rubles. But

he says his generation will protest, will question, will demand. They won't be gun meat. I decide to stop bitching about my problems.

Back to Moscow. Write a bunch of stories for Serge to send by fax. Do my laundry in hotel bathtub. Nice surprise in the coffee shop. Waiter almost smiles at me. He says "Eggs?" I say "Omelet?" He says, "No problem." Then an American businessman comes. He's a big-dealer. He's going to straighten people out, right now. He demands freshly squeezed orange juice. They don't have it. Grapefruit juice? Nyet. Apple juice? Nyet. He continues through guava, mango and passion fruit. All nyets. Now he's mad. "Now listen Charlie, this is what I want. I want a Western omelet. Chopped ham, green and red peppers, potatoes. Understand? And rye toast. And some fresh fruit." I am fascinated by this. The waiter hasn't blinked at the rudeness. After twenty minutes the guy gets his breakfast. Two fried eggs, over hard, and a green apple on a crystal plate.

Well, here's another fine mess you've gotten me into, Stalin. We're in Yalta, where Roosevelt, Stalin and Churchill carved up postwar Europe and Stalin ate Churchill's lunch.

We were supposed to have reservations at a magnificent tourist hotel overlooking the Crimean Sea. When we got there, no rooms. Serge bribed a desk clerk and got the straight dope. Seven hundred members of the Russian Mafia have arrived, unannounced, over the past two days and taken over most of the two thousand rooms. Everyone else with a room, including seventy outraged Americans, was turfed out. A lot of them slept in the lobby, in the bars. We have lunch in a co-op restaurant. The owner, Viktor, says the crime rate is terrible. He tells Serge he is terrified the Mafia will demand protection money, maybe just take his place.

Instead of a comfy hotel, they put us into an old railway flat, one long room partitioned, two miles uphill from the beach. There is no food so Serge goes foraging. He comes back at 11 P.M. with a hunk of sausage, milk, coffee and a watermelon. A day later we

move, farther uphill to a summer camp populated mostly by Germans who spend all day polishing their cars. I hate it here. So does Serge. The strain is showing on him. He has been drinking triple brandies, bumming my smokes and his face has broken out in pimples. He has tried to have us rerouted to Leningrad, but Moscow nixes him. He has begun to refer to us as Detainees 36 and 37. Moscow arranges for us to have lunch at a hotel restaurant on the beach if we arrive before the tour groups come in. Tables are pre-set so we stuff our pockets with hard-boiled eggs, tomatoes and cucumbers from the relish trays. Ever try to walk out of a restaurant with dignity when you have a cucumber in your pocket? I have told Serge that if I'd been here during peace talks, the war would still be on.

On our last day in Yalta, the waitress who had served us four days in a row demands advance payment. She doesn't like us. She thinks we are The Ones Who Do Not Belong. Serge says something to her and she backed off. I asked what he said. He had told her to go to hell. Unusual for him to have his big argument so early in the day.

At last we are out of Yalta after five hellish days. We drive to Simferopol airport, catch flight to Riga. We have no reservations in Riga. Serge says his Moscow protocol man should be shot with a ball of his own cranial fat.

Twenty-minute cab drive from Riga airport and we are at the Latvija Hotel, which seems too good to be true. There is food here! There is courtesy. People smile! Toilets flush! There is brewed coffee! At our first buffet breakfast, Serge eats six slices of bread, two Danish, stacks of cheese and cold cuts, marinated onions. I have eggs, pancakes and sausage.

As in the other two Baltic states, there is much talk of independence here. Serge says we might be here at a historic time. He's nervous, too. Latvians don't like Russians.

Latvia was founded by the Germans in the twelfth century. In all that time, they have had just twenty years of full independence. But in that short time they created an auto industry and became world leaders in camera technology.

Heard a disturbance outside at midnight. Cars, banners, people dressed in white, police vehicles, bullhorns bellowing orders. I thought it was a freedom march. It was the start of a marathon run. But we attended a rally where the Latvian flag was flown openly for the first time since the early forties. And we visited the offices of the Popular Front independence group. Their spokesman spoke perfect English. He told me tens of thousands of people in the three republics had linked hands in a gesture hundreds of miles long. He also asked me how I figured the Canucks would do. That one baffled me.

Back in Moscow for countdown to return home. Wouldn't have missed it. Serge and I saw a street guy sitting at a card table piled high with light bulbs, supposedly a deficit product. He has customers lined up the street. Serge talks to him and comes back roaring. He tells me, "They are burned-out light bulbs." And explains.

"Nobody can buy light bulbs. If you work for the state or the party and the bulb burns out at your desk, you have to phone the building superintendent to get a replacement. Now, this man is selling burned-out bulbs for five kopeks. These people will take them back to their offices. They will unscrew a good bulb, put it in their pocket and replace it with this burned-out bulb. The superintendent will replace that bulb with a new one. The worker now has a good bulb in his lamp and one in his pocket. which he takes home. And this man here is making a five-kopek profit on bulbs that don't work. Everyone wins. Do you like it?"

I loved it.

Last night. I'm in the Rossya Hotel, the world's biggest. There are twenty six wickets for signing in, but then you have to go outside half a block to the elevators and no one to help with luggage. Serge says I look tired and I am, but he must be totally bagged, what with all the responsibility and putting up with my bitching.

August 29. Airborne and climbing at 3:04 P.M. Moscow time. I'm going home. All I can think of is dropping my bags in my apartment, drinking cold milk, eating peanut butter toast and sleeping forever.

155

Before we left the hotel, Serge insisted we follow a Russian custom: Sit quietly for three minutes trying to think of anything undone, unchecked or unpacked. Nothing. So we took our last drive up Leningradski Prospekt to the airport. Over lunch Serge said something insightful. He said, "The feelings you will have about us are irritation and admiration."

Then he hauled me to the front of another long lineup. The customs guy was so spaced by Serge's ballsiness that he helped me climb over a barrier even though I was one document short. Blat to the very end.

But everything finished in such a rush that I barely had time to reach back and shake Serge's hand.

I hate second thoughts because they always occur an hour too late. But on second thought, I wish I had hugged him.

Chapter 13

Then I came home, back to established routine, back to the Big Diary.

Sept. 1. I slept for two days and went back to my office. Individual colleagues, reporters and deskmen, were generous with praise for the stuff I filed from the USSR. Management was less than enthusiastic; they seem to be in limbo. That's because of the notice on the bulletin board. Gord Fisher is gone as of October 1. Mixed emotions on that one. He did some good things here, some baffling things. He's going to a better job, he's certainly on his way up the Southam chain and he'll be the hell out of my hair. He's the only manager I have had who interfered with my column.

Sept. 2. Wrote, then totally rewrote, a piece on events in the Baltic states. Wrote it straight, as requested, then put some firsthand personality in it. Much better. McRanor liked second version. He's said to be the next managing editor.

Sept. 3. Talked to Haysom. He says Fisher move was in the works for a long time. He says he has no regrets about moving to *Province*, even though he'd be heir apparent at our place. He figures McRanor will get a title, possibly exec-assistant to Hills, with Macrae as A.M.E. Suspects M.E. may be brought in from outside. Please God, no.

Sept. 5. Started plowing through mound of Soviet notebooks, rough notes of twenty or so interviews. Wrote three stories, chatted with Hills, but still no debriefing with editorial board. I've told

them I don't think Gorbachev is going to make it. Eyes glaze over.

Sept. 8. Spoke briefly with Frank Baker. Poor bugger has pancreatic cancer. It's terminal. They give him three to six months. He's taking it well. But his voice has that reediness I've heard before in people who didn't make it.

Sept. 12. Have been pounding out Soviet copy. Was supposed to have two pages Friday and a long analysis piece Saturday. But Gord is fixated on the East Berlin exodus story. He circulated memo saying, "Before Boyd gets two pages I want East Berlin story hammered." So I get one page Saturday, one Monday. Today's rumours: Rutter for Ottawa column; Macrae for M.E. I can live with Macrae.

Sept. 14. Didn't go in. Big mistake. Heard that photo desk was laying out special Soviet pages, butchering my copy to make room for stock photos from library. Phoned Fralic and whined at her to do something.

Sept. 15. Fralic came through. Cuts to copy restored, page looks pretty damned good.

Sept. 16. *Province* converts to new format Monday. Haysom says he wants to put sports on back page, British tab style. But that page brings in $1 million a year in advertising. He says he has three to four months of hard surgery ahead to get things going his way.

Sept. 18. Memo says Jamie and I move into our new office Oct. 2. I snuck in to have a look. Ran into Hills and Paddy Sherman. Sherman said he liked my Soviet stuff. Said, "By God, there's life in the old guy yet." In this business, that's a compliment.

Sept. 20. Spoke to Mike McRanor about space problems on second front. Suggested I wouldn't complain if I was cut to three columns a week, freeing up some space. He was intrigued.

Sept. 21. Mike took three-column week suggestion to management meeting. He thinks they'll buy it.

Sept. 22. Got totally screwed up on Richmond ringroad on way to have coffee with Lloyd Axworthy. Lost. Drove back to office and did telephone interview. Feel like jerk.

Sept. 24. Four of us went on weekend retreat at Westminster Abbey. Didn't sleep worth a hoot but feel a bit refreshed. Some

good rap sessions with the monks. They're very tuned into alcohol problems. Back to find McRanor confirmed as executive editor, Rutter as foreign affairs columnist. If he doesn't get a reasonable travel budget it confirms what we all know — they want him to resign. Trevor to be exec. ed. of editorial pages. Do I sense a political shift, from Rutter's liberalism to a more right-of-centre position? Apparently, Nick wants to endorse Socreds in next election. Wouldn't happen with Rutter in there.

Sept. 25. Big going-away bash for Fisher at tennis club. Booze flowed. He made fairly gracious farewell speech. Poor guy looks rough. Apparently, he and Hills have been drinking long lunches. Gord got over-matched.

Sept. 26. Half the brass didn't make it in. Suffering from Fisher party. Amateurs!

Sept. 29. Long lunch at Peppi's with Gary Bannerman. We swapped interviews. He looks much better than last time we met and seems to have health back. Told me he never was hooked on booze, though he could drain two bottles of Scotch a day. During lunch he was called away to take a call from the premier. Nice touch. Beat hell out of my pair of deuces.

Oct. 2. Scott Macrae confirmed as M.E. I like it. Waiting for second shoe to drop — Fralic for city editor. She says she has newsroom enemies who might form ABF movement: Anyone But Fralic.

Oct. 3. Three Socred backbenchers, including Doug Mowat, resigned from caucus to sit as independents. Another shiv in Vander Zalm's back, but he doesn't seem to be aware that he's bleeding to death. Had to go back in after that news came in to do a replacement column.

Oct. 4. Breakfast with Tom Perry. He doesn't realize that the way things are going, he could be our next health minister. Got to play with my new word processor. I have decided to call it Spot. Went to Jack Munro's book launch. Ghosted by Jane O'Hara, it could be surprise seller of the year. Who but Munro ever said "bullshit" to Prince Philip?

Oct. 5. I'm bowled over by the money they seem to have spent on

the new columnists' office. First cabin all the way. Up to Bishop's for lunch with Julius Weinstein, eighty-year-old writer who won an Oscar for the *Casablanca* screenplay. Interesting old bird, frail, deaf, but witty company.

Oct. 9. Talked to Linda as she packed for a four-month stay in Iowa. She expects a hard winter. She's still hurting over split with Mike. Poor kid, she can't accept that it's over.

Oct. 10. Scott came in and delicately asked if I'd mind cutting back to three columns a week. I humbly agreed to, as if I'd never heard the suggestion before. But Archie, Pete and Nicole are mad as hell at me for suggesting it. I keep trying to tell them it will prolong their careers. That doesn't help their insecurities. Laura called. She wants me to lend her $50,000 so she can buy Neal out of his share of the townhouse and get a divorce. My family!

Oct. 14. Lions gave up fifty-one points in Calgary. This is the last year for the franchise for sure.

Oct. 15. Snaffled a copy of the outside consultant's report on management-staff relations. Some good stuff in it — tough evaluation of deteriorating physical plant, lack of desks for reporters, unwillingness of editors to praise reporters — but there is too much focus on the paper's "vision." If the vision isn't to get a readable paper on the street every day and the paycheques out every two weeks, someone is playing out of tune.

Oct.16. Nick put up a very blunt, forceful bulletin board response to the consultant's report on staff morale. Lot of staffers can't figure him out. They don't see that he's so cocky, so utterly self-confident, that mention of staff morale doesn't intimidate him. Fisher would have taken it personally; Larsen would have panicked. Nick copes.

Oct 18. Pete McMartin did himself, the paper and the trade proud. In California to cover the World Series, he got caught in the terrible San Francisco earthquake. Despite horrendous problems, he filed three terrific stories and kept updating all day. Not only does he have a phenomenal horseshoe up his ass — wherever he goes, stories break — he's also a great reporter. He works in the crunch.

Oct 19. Good AA meeting at R.C.'s. Subject was letting go, which permitted a few of us to blow off steam about the problems our kids continue to cause us, simply because we permit them to do so. Fact is, we insist on it just by hanging on, refusing to let them go.

Oct. 26. Got a good column on a phone tip. Young Haida kid seriously hurt in stabbing on Robson Street. Appears members of an Oriental gang jumped him for no good reason. Got story from his co-workers and good co-operation from contacts in Major Crime. If he dies, there may be murder charges against as many as six gang members. City side didn't have a word on it, didn't seem much interested. The new reality of life in Big Town.

Nov 3. Lousy day, great day. Out in thunderous rain to have sushi with Robert Fulghum, the Seattle preacher-philosopher who's the hottest thing between covers these days. He's the guy who first attracted attention with his pamphlet about having learned everything he had to know in kindergarten. His first book had 1.2 million sales in hard cover; 2.5 million print run in paperback comes out next month. His second book has sold 700,000 in two months. Both books in NY *Times* best-seller list. He's going to get seriously rich.

Nov 5. Talked to Lenny, Lisa and Laura. All seem well. But why do I have to do the calling?

Nov 6. A.E.M. calls to say G.M. is off the wagon, locked up in his house, drinking, not answering phone. Dodger and I took a run over, couldn't rouse him if he was there. He's been owly the last couple of weeks.

Nov. 8. Stones and I got to G.M. tonight. He's been drinking for six days; started right after meeting at my place. (Something we said?) He laughed, he sobbed, he raged, he did somersaults, whole nine yards. Seen it all before. We hid his car key, dumped what booze we could find, got him to bed. Strange, we had to get to him drunk to see him let his guard down and admit his fears.

Nov. 14. Chaired panel on substance abuse in North Van, with five professional counsellors giving their best shot. But something incredible happened. Three high school girls got up and told their stories. All have kicked and are peer counsellors at their schools.

One girl spoke through tears and stayed with it. She said if drug use doesn't stop, she fears that "Someday there won't be any people, just things controlled by drugs." What an impact she made.

Nov. 20. Private lunch with Allen Gotlieb, former Canadian ambassador to Washington. I had heard he was a bitch to interview but he wasn't bad, answered most of our questions, talked around others adroitly.

Nov. 21. Frank Baker bought the farm today. Died just before 3, pretty much on schedule with the time the doctors had given him. Frank lived most of his life garishly, theatrically. But he knew he was dying and he did it with dignity.

Nov. 22. Driving through town on a spectacularly clear, icy day, I reflected on how good it is to be alive. Immediately felt guilty. Frank B. isn't alive. An overreaction, surely.

Nov. 27. As I hear it, Scott Macrae and Hills want Gary Mason as city editor. He likes Victoria bureau job, wasn't going to apply. They asked him to apply. Under pressure, he did. His appointment was to be posted last Friday. But one of the consultants that floats around here like feeding perch offered opinion that Mason is the wrong guy because the newsroom staff don't know him except as a byline out of Victoria. Last Friday, Macrae goes to Victoria to tell him it's all off. Mason's furious; he'd been making moving plans. Mucho egg covers many faces.

Nov. 29. Had studio portrait taken of the family. Christmas present for Mom. Amazing how well we get along when we get together.

Nov. 30. Did an opinion column on Judge van der Hoop decision. Always nervous about writing on judges. Many, many false starts.

Dec. 1. Peter Butler called. In that outboard motor voice he said my van der Hoop column was sound, rational and logical. Only criticism — and he said it would have hurt my argument in a courtroom — was that I let my own prejudices show in the brief rant about drunkenness as an argument for clemency. Interesting comment from an unexpected source. He added that he's impressed with Nick Hills; says he stands up for his journalists.

Dec. 3. Ran into Annis Stukus at picture shoot for a celebrity pix

book. Stuke was wearing the leather helmet he wore in the 1938 Grey Cup game.

Dec. 4. We made ourselves look silly today. With a light Monday paper, we devoted almost all of page three to the fact that we raised $75,000 at Sunday's garage sale. Meanwhile the Telethon raised $3 million and we didn't mention it, not a word.

Dec. 5. Attended two-hour session with Angus Reid, detailing results of our $125,000 readership poll. Says our circulation target is the reader called the Literary Inquisitor. They read. They like quality writing. They don't like gimmicks. One bit of gloom: Parton outpolls me in four of five reader groups. Hills, Macrae and McRanor took turns apologizing for the Gary Mason screw-up and announced he is, for sure, the city editor.

Dec. 9. Despite toothache, attended Norval Morriseau's gallery show on Granville. His work is powerful, stunning. Harvey Oberfeld of BCTV was there, trying to decide which of two $3,000 pieces he was going to buy as an investment.

Dec. 11. Went to Nancy's support group meeting. What came out is that she really doesn't think she knows me and wants a closer relationship. It's not asking much; must work on it.

Dec. 12. Tooth still pounding at me. Met Lloyd Axworthy at a house on Keith Road. Told him it was freezing out, I had a miserable toothache, so would he please give me something and not play around. He was great about it. Declared himself in as contender for Liberal leadership, which makes for a Canadian scoop in tomorrow's paper.

Dec. 13. On antibiotics and painkillers. Socreds must be, too. They lost Oak Bay by-election. That's six in a row. That's the end of them, perhaps for the millennium.

Dec. 17. Have booked off until after Christmas. Phoned Mom, congratulated her on her eightieth birthday. Called Lesley in Toronto but her husband answered. I'm not paying long distance toll to talk to him.

Dec. 20. Well into my annual pre-Christmas hairball mode. Morose, restless.

Dec. 22. Solved a problem brilliantly. Paid Laura $20 to come over and wrap my Christmas presents, except hers. One less chance to go Christmas bonkers. A lonely call from Wally D. Said he heard Lenny and I are going to Chartwell for Christmas dinner. Said he envied us. I invited him to join us, but he declined.

Dec. 25. Gnarly in the morning. Not crazy about any of my presents (no sled, no pony, no mature behaviour). Great time at dinner at Chartwell. Table beside fireplace, Lenny most impressed. Felt hairball recede one minute into Boxing Day.

Dec. 26. Worked like mad all morning getting food ready for family gathering. Will never do pot-stickers from scratch again. But it was worth it, all four generations together and Linda called from Iowa to fill out the card.

Dec. 30. Dickens of an experience. In five minutes while walking through Park Royal, ran into Gord Fisher, Scott Macrae and Ian Haysom. Editors past, present and future?

Dec. 31. Ryan and Shaun will stay with me tonight while Lisa and Kevin party. Am wondering if I want to do another journal for 1990. All this one has proved is that my life is dull, dull!

Chapter 14

It was in the nineties that I began to get the hang of my job. After forty years of poking and pecking, I made the jump from being a pretty adequate columnist to being a pretty good columnist.

I wouldn't want to leave the incorrect impression that I am a slow learner or winsomely modest. I am neither. It's just that it took me four decades to discover that the most essential factor of opinion writing is confidence. And that comes slowly and from two directions — from without and from within. Despite whatever exalted position the job may seem to hold, I don't know many columnists who are not insecure, marginally paranoid and who haven't, sometime during their career, had to deal with a confidence crisis. Their egos can be shattered like crystal by the slightest vibration of disapproval and magically repaired by a nod of agreement, a whisper of praise.

For a bad stretch in the eighties, I felt I had lost the confidence of my editors at the *Sun*. There was second guessing, quibbling, undermining, and I let it get to me. In the face of second-guessing by my editors, I began to second-guess them, at least to anticipate what might work with them. So I started, on at least a subliminal level, to write for editors instead of writing for readers. When you do that you lose all around. You lose spontaneity, you lose the voice you have established in your space in the paper. You lose your balls. You don't take chances: you play safe, hoping that what you write won't prompt another of those next-day memos on coloured paper that start out, "I had a little problem with your column today . . ."

That's especially difficult to choke down when the executive people writing the memos have no broad, proven experience in column writing but still want to teach you how to do it.

So I wrote in a joyless funk for a couple of years until time and circumstance gave back what I had lost. There were more executive changes at the *Sun*. The atmosphere changed. When Nick Hills came in as editor-in-chief, he sensed or was told (I suspect he was told) that at least three of the columnists he was inheriting had been wounded and needed some patching up. Hills did great work, and it didn't take much. He sent out glowing memos. He made a point of telling us verbally that he liked our work. And he built a spiffy new office, sparing no expense, for Jamie Lamb, Trev Lautens and me. He sent me to the Soviet Union, a gem of an assignment.

Hills didn't survive his own generosity. He spent like a caliph, on long lunches downtown, on costly readership surveys, on overseas news services in his attempt to make us look and read like *The Times* of London, on hiring new columnists in an attempt to box the ideological compass. When he had just about exhausted the editorial treasury, he was fired by the general manager, Stu Noble. Just before they nailed him, Hills did the only unsavoury thing I recall from his reign. In an attempt to delay his own beheading, he axed managing editor Scott Macrae, a damned loyal and conscientious administrator, a good handler of people and a continual writer of praise-laden memos to columnists.

Hills left with a nice severance package that he took with him to England, and his departure brought my pal Ian Haysom back from the *Province* as our new editor-in-chief in February, 1991 (where he stayed until July 4, 1995). After a long and costly search, a former *Sun* reporter, Scott Honeyman, was brought in from Ottawa as managing editor, and the hugely talented and wonderfully witty Shelley Fralic moved up to deputy managing editor.

Don Babick was brought in from Edmonton as publisher of the *Sun* and *Province* and as Pacific Press CEO. He was a godsend. Short, pink-faced and cherubic-looking, Babick in fact was a hard-ball player. He battled the most feather-bedding trade unions, elim-

inated entire departments, cut costs by contracting out where possible, stopped the overall financial bleeding just short of collapse and may have saved the paper in its worst crisis in history.

This was a team I was happy to play for. I knew the editors well, I knew they could write and I respected them. I reported directly to Fralic on a daily basis, had little to do with Honeyman, except on an informal bull-session basis and didn't push or exploit my long friendship with Haysom beyond what was comfortable for both of us. Haysom is not a memo-writer. If he has something to say, good or bad, he is more likely to yell it down the hallway. In fact, I think he manages to some extent by withholding praise. But I knew him well enough to know that no flak is good flak.

And I credit him with writing one hall-of-fame memo. During the 1994 Stanley Cup final between the Vancouver Canucks and the New York Rangers, *Sun* sports editor Brad Zeimer complained that the *Province* was committing more manpower to the coverage than we were. He sent a memo to Haysom that said, "Number of *Province* staffers in New York, six. Number of *Sun* staffers in New York, four." Haysom's reply was, "Number of sports editors beginning to piss me off, one."

Whatever value there is in executive praise, there was always a newsroom balance that kept things in perspective. I got my cold water directly from sports columnist Archie McDonald — "I read your column today, Boyd. Keep up the adequate work" — and from newsroom reporter Wyng Chow — "So tell me, Boyd, when do you figure to come out of your losing streak?"

The nineties was my happiest time at the *Sun*. The spirit was good, there was a sense of direction and the paper was lively. I'm still not convinced the move to the morning market was a wise one. I still think we would have been a bigger winner putting out our nineties paper under our nineties management for the evening market. But it's an unproveable opinion.

I think the best column I wrote in the nineties was one about Jamie Bulger, the little British boy abducted and brutally murdered

by two other boys seemingly as a lark or an act of boredom. I did-
n't want to write it. I had a hard time writing it. But as you read it,
I think it will explain something about the column process. I wrote
this for the November 26, 1993 paper:

"All of us who work in and around the *Sun* newsroom have a leg
up on the world. At the touch of a keyboard button, we can call up all
the news of the world, a day before you read it, in a volume one hundred times greater than we can put into a single edition of the paper.

"We can wade through the thickness of the news, we can bathe
in its steamy heat, which boils out of a gushing tap that has no Off
setting.

"But yesterday was the first time in a month that I read a Jamie
Bulger story. During the month-long trial that was a headliner all
over the world, I didn't read the daily flood of stories. I wouldn't
read them. The truth is, I couldn't.

"I would try to read the stories about the poor wee boy in
Liverpool, abducted and brutally beaten by two incomprehensible
ten year olds, deliberately left dead on railway tracks, his body to be
cut in half by a train, and I would run out of the ability to read any
more. I would feel my muscles and nerves bunching up in knots of
rage, and the beginnings of low-grade nausea.

"Forty-three years in the news business and I couldn't read a
news story in my own paper.

"Partly, I am sure, it is because I have six grandchildren, the
youngest a sweet little boy the same age Jamie would be.

"But I think more compelling, more forbidding than that, was a
single line of testimony I heard early on. I think it came out during
preliminary police interviews with the two boys charged with, and
now convicted of, Jamie Bulger's murder. It was related that, after
the two boys had abducted Jamie, and then kicked and dragged
him three miles across town to a railway cut, and began systemati-
cally to beat him to death, 'he kept trying to get up . . .'

"That was what did it to me. Amid all the terror and horror of
this event, even after he had been beaten to the ground, been par-
tially disrobed, after the bigger boys had painted his face and began

to pound and smash him with rocks and metal bars, little Jamie Bulger kept trying to get to his feet, to save himself, but the beating continued until Jamie was beyond getting up, ever again.

"After that, until yesterday, I couldn't handle any more details.

"The trial has been resolved but the Bulger story remains beyond understanding, such is the unimaginable horror of it. To even begin to understand it, two ten year olds, stalking, taking and coldly beating a two year old to death, we may even have to redefine our understanding of the word evil, since that was a word used in the judgement. Now evil is spawning more 'evil', as Jamie Bulger's uncle threatens that the Bulger family will, in turn, kill the two convicted boys if they are ever released from prison.

"How long does it take to become wicked? Is evil born in us and washed out by the happiness of childhood, or is it absorbed by a terrible osmosis? Or has a new strain of wickedness come to us, like some demonic spores from outer space?

"We can absorb, or learn to block out the murder in Bosnia, to set ourselves apart from the casual murders of children and babies in drive-by shootings in the gang-ruled and drug-fueled ghettos in the United States.

"But we have nothing, nothing at all, with which to compare and perhaps rationalize, even superficially, Jamie Bulger's murder. It is as if a whole new box of hell has been opened and the imps and demons overwhelm us.

" 'He kept trying to get up . . .'

"Is this the new generation? The late Graham Greene wrote in *The Power and the Glory*, 'There is always one moment in childhood when the door opens and lets the future in.'

"Were the two convicted predators born evil, or did they ingest evil from the world around them? Social critic Brian Aldiss wrote, 'When childhood dies its corpses are called adults and they enter society, one of the politer names for Hell. That is why we dread children, even as we love them. They show us the state of our own decay.'

"As you weep for Jamie Bulger, weep for humanity."

Here is an irony to wrestle with. I wouldn't mind being remembered for that column, but it won't happen. It's the kind of piece people talk about for a few days and then put out of their minds because it is unpleasant and not useful to the reader.

If I'm remembered for anything, it is going to be for that damned potato recipe.

In the late eighties, I wrote a light, whimsical column about potatoes: their history, their uses, how much I liked them. I particularly focused on the tiny new potatoes we get every spring from the Fraser Valley, and how smart shoppers burrow down to the bottom of the market box to get at the tiniest of them. I included a cooking method I had worked out, boiling the little gems in a saucepan with a tight cover, with nothing but butter and unpeeled garlic cloves. No water. Just lots of butter and lots of garlic. Takes about twenty minutes over medium heat, shaking the pot frequently. Gorgeous.

There was no response for a year, which was long enough for scores of readers to lose the column. I began getting letters, asking me to repeat the instructions. So did our Foods section. Sunday evenings, I would get frantic phone calls from people. Their steaks were on the barbecue or their roast was in the oven and they had forgotten how to cook the new potatoes. At least half of them thought the absence of water was a printer's error. It still happens, every season. I have never had more response to a column.

Journalism is the horse I rode on and I never expected to fall off clutching a gunny sack of spuds.

Chapter 15

Back in the days of clattering typewriters, pulpy copy paper and hot type, I knew as much as I had to know about the process of producing a newspaper, the miraculous endeavour of creating an entirely new product six times a week and scrapping that product at the end of every working day.

What I knew was that if I wrote something down and handed it to someone else, they would put it the paper. They might yell and curse and call me an illiterate blockhead, but they would usually put what I wrote down in the paper. Beyond that, I didn't ask.

With the possible exception of spotting forest fires from a remote wooden tower, writing is the loneliest work there is. It is just you doing it in a vacuum. You can't ask for help. You can't yell out, "Hey, come here and help me lift this sentence. Grab that end." Or, "Can I borrow your vocabulary for half a sec?"

Musicians can get away with playing two-handed piano, but if two writers sat down to the same typewriter or computer keyboard, one would in short order kill the other, and then write about it.

Book writing is the worst. When I write a column and it gets past the copy desk and the senior editors and into the paper the next day, I know I've done well. The fact that it made it without someone yelling at me is about as much approval as one gets on a newspaper. But with a book, you write day after day with no approval. The pages pile up but there is no reassurance that you're moving it in the right direction. And you don't show the work to

anyone lest the silly damned fool suggest you are moving in the wrong direction.

> "No one but a blockhead ever wrote, except for money."
> *Samuel Johnson*

It's hard work, too, hard physical work. When I finish writing eight hundred or three thousand words, my body hurts. I have to get up and stretch as if I've been toting lump coal for a few hours. John Gregory Dunne, the American writer, says writing is like laying pipe. It's even worse on those wretched days when the pipes won't fit together. My mentor Paul St. Pierre says the one blessing of writing is that there's no heavy lifting. Easy for him to say, he who is seldom cursed with leaden sentences.

I think writing is as close as a man can get to the experience of childbearing. It is just you and that thing growing inside of you. There are those bilious mornings when you don't, you just *don't*, want to go to the desk. There may be bloating and swollen ankles. The months of discomfort pass and then there is that final birthing effort at the end of term. ("Push!") Even writers get postnatal blues. There may be an unwillingness to give the little piece of new life up to a publisher. He may not treat it tenderly, bring it up the way you would.

> "Writing a book is a horrible, exhausting struggle, like a long bout of some powerful illness. One would never undertake such a thing if one were not driven by some demon whom one can neither resist nor understand." *George Orwell*

Still, it can be good fun and rewarding work if you can be satisfied with the enjoyment and satisfaction of putting enough carefully chosen words in proper sequence to make a cogent sentence, and enough of those into crisp paragraphs, and so on. Writers are not like professional athletes. You are not likely to see a writer spike his mouse and boogie around the room after creating an apt metaphor

But I myself have been heard to utter "hah" after getting off a good line. Anything further leads to self-aggrandizement, which is dangerous in this profession. It's a pity someone hasn't created a computer program that compliments the writer from time to time. Surely they could get someone who writes the dialogue for porn films to program soft computer moans and stuff like, "Oh . . . yes . . . more . . . you're so good . . . don't stop." It would surely brighten the writer's bleakest day, prop up his flaccid confidence, and I'm almost certain it would not lead to self-abuse.

While this may sound simplistic, the trick is to sit down and do it. Don't overcomplicate the mechanics of writing, which are making the mind and the fingers move in unison. Avoid cold starts. Don't sit down to the writing desk unless you have at least your first paragraph mapped out and edited in your head. With any luck, that first paragraph will create the momentum to the second. When Robert Benchley was writing a column for a New York newspaper, he frequently came to work hung-over and empty of ideas. His kick-start of a cold motor was to roll the paper in confidently, crack his knuckles once and type the word "The." That would lead to a topic and a column. One day he came in looking like death on a soda cracker, went through his fail safe procedure, typed a few more words, got up, put his coat on and left. His colleagues, aware of his trick, came over to see what he had written. He had typed "The" and then "hell with it." He never came back.

"I love being a writer. What I can't stand is the paper-work."

Peter De Vries

I could never help anyone write a great novel or a memorable short story, but I know how to write a 750-word column. Again, the trick is to have the first and the last paragraphs written in your head before booting up the machine. All that has to be filled in is the seven hundred or so words of the middle. Whip up a jam of chocolate ganache to put between the layers, as it were, and, Bob's your uncle, there's another column.

I have also found that when I freeze in front of the word processor, I can get the engine warmed by going to a different room and writing in longhand. A cold machine may be intimidating, but by long familiarity, pen and paper are our more obedient servants.

"Writing isn't hard. You just take pen to paper and write down whatever occurs to you. The writing is easy, it's the occurring that's hard." *Stephen Leacock*

I'll for sure get snotty letters for letting this out, but there are only four or five types of columns. Get the hang of them and you can be hailed as a pundit.

There is, most commonly, the Thumbsucker. This is the heavy opinion column, also called the Think Piece. All it requires is a furrowed brow and an impressive list of statistics, which any librarian can dig up for you. Writers of Thumbsuckers invariably work in state capitals and are secretly loathed.

The Walkabout is just what it implies. It is a Thumbsucker with atmosphere, birds and children. One must get up and outside to research a Walkabout. When I am blanked, I put on a coat and walk over the Granville Street Bridge and come back and write with a furrowed brow that the junkies and rummies and hookers are taking over the streets again. My *Sun* colleague Jamie Lamb wrote terrific Walkabout columns. He has good young legs and knows every damned bird in the trees.

The Bow and Arrow is usually written with the eyes shut. The writer nocks a brand new, never-before-used idea into his bow, shoots it straight up and hopes it doesn't hurt anyone on its way down.

On a dull news day in 1993, I noticed that the cherry blossoms had burst forth, as they had done every spring since I could remember. No surprise, no news story there. But I wrote an appreciation of them, added a bit of factual research, put a piece into the bow and shot it into the air. The response was phenomenal. My

phone was jammed with callers who just wanted to say, "Thank you for the cherry blossom column."

The Wife/Cute-Kid-Said column is beneath contempt.

One category of column that is best handled gingerly and with deep consideration is the What-in-the-Name-of Christ-is-This-All-About piece. This is the column which brings the purple-faced editor-in-chief into your office two hours after deadline, clutching the paper and screaming, "What in the name of Christ is this all about?"

When hockey czar Alan Eagleson was under heavy legal fire in 1994, I wrote a column about him and added, in a grumbling way, that my paper was not covering the story adequately, and that I had to read the Toronto *Globe & Mail* to keep current. Next morning, Haysom met me at the door. His face was the colour of a chimney brick. He chewed me out, starting at my head and working down. He said I had gone over the line and that he was "pissed off, big time." I had broken two of his rules: I had criticized my own paper and I had praised a competitor in our own circulation market. The outburst was impressive. I never did it again.

This may be followed a day later by what is known as the I-May-Have-Erred column.

At the *Sun*, at least, I tried to maintain what I call the Dead Beat. I'm talking about obituaries. Reporters and many columnists hate doing them, makes them feel clammy. For that reason, the once-honoured art of obit writing has sunk to a dismal depth in Canadian newspapers. I have written so many of them that a few people have actually tried to reserve time with me. "Promise to do mine?," they ask, with no squeamishness at all. My friend, the brilliant Southam reporter Patrick Nagle, advised me to read the classified obituaries every day. "A dozen potential columns every day," he guaranteed me. They require a lot of work, a lot of checking with people who knew the deceased, a lot of doggedness in digging out the funny, the compelling anecdotes that mark every life. They don't have to be — in fact should not be — maudlin. And it's

going to be the last chance you'll have to write about the person in a timely fashion.

I have been writing for a living since 1951. Every dollar I have earned in that time came from writing, except for what I made in radio. I don't regard my radio money as earnings. I was so bad I regard it as theft. Most of the stuff I have written has been accepted and printed. Most of it has been sold to the small-potatoes market of newspapers and magazines. I have never had to hire a brace of good lawyers to help me negotiate the film rights to one of my pieces. By the same token, I have been spoiled. I have never had to plead or threaten to get someone to at least read what I have written, nor have I had to endure the heartbreak, the humiliation, the discouragement of rejection letters from publishing houses that may have never read more than the first five pages of a manuscript before passing its death sentence. I have heard it said, and it makes sense, that the worst mistake young writers make is enclosing a stamped and self-addressed envelope with a submitted manuscript. Wiser old writers say the envelope creates in the editor a temptation that is too strong to resist.

The essence of good writing is originality. Think of what makes you stop while you are reading, back up and reread a sentence that has delighted you. The writer has put before you a description so utterly apt that you can see what he or she is describing. Or has created a metaphor or a simile you have never heard before. That newness, the freshness, is what delights your senses, just as compellingly as a piece of radiantly fresh fish, fragrant with the perfume of just-picked herbs. If the waiter asks if the fish seemed fresh and you reply that it was near perfect, you are just a discerning diner. If you reply that if it has been any fresher it would have been insolent, you may be a potential writer.

So it is essential to work at the style of your writing. The sweetness of writing is in unwrapping a fresh, green metaphor, one that is all yours. For God's sake, avoid the tiresome simile, the trite cliche you have heard a hundred times and use only because it comes easily. Don't use cliches. Avoid them like the plague. Don't

touch them with a ten-foot pole. Follow this advice, give it 110 per cent and you'll be pleased as punch. Believe-you me.

If you aren't a writer yet, but hope to become one, start keeping a daily journal. No matter that you think your life is dull or empty of swashbuckling adventure; a record of it is an investment in experience that will eventually pay dividends. If you happen to see squirrels and chipmunks scurrying around Stanley Park, dodging cars and storing food, write an immediate description in your journal. It may fill a detailed page in a book you write ten years from now. Same thing for an automobile accident you might witness. If you eat raw oysters for the first time, describe your sensations. They may become valuable in retrospect. If a street crazy punches you out for not having spare change, you may want to forget the experience as soon as possible. You would be better off putting the pain, the outrage, the humiliation down in words that could illuminate a knowledgeable passage in a future book. It will be much harder to imagine and create such an event without that useful, though painful, experience.

And, of course, you must read. Reading is the best route to writing. Read every day. Read voraciously. Read analytically. Try to understand why you enjoy a particular phrase or sentence. It may be simply the perfect use of a single word. If you read or hear a great phrase, write it down. Use it as your own in two months time. That is not stealing, it's redistribution and it is allowed.

> "If a writer has to rob his mother, he will not hesitate. 'Ode to a Grecian Urn' is worth any number of old ladies."
>
> *William Faulkner*

Read Hemingway. He was a drunkard, a braggart, a bully and a liar. But he could write. If you can't read everything he wrote, at least read *The Old Man and the Sea* to see what perfect craftsmanship is all about. His first sentence is a glittering emerald, perfectly cut and polished. In twenty-seven words, Hemingway establishes the character, the locale, the character and the conflict. That is economy to

be worshipped. Many writers would have taken five pages to relate what Hemingway did in one perfect sentence.

Whiskey won't help. There have been too many bad movies about booze-soaked reporters and novelists. Just because piss tanks like Edgar Allan Poe, Ambrose Bierce, Theodore Dreiser, Hart Crane, Sinclair Lewis, Eugene O'Neill, Dorothy Parker, F. Scott Fitzgerald, Ring Lardner, Ernest Hemingway, John O'Hara, William Faulkner, John Steinbeck, Dashiell Hammett, Thomas Wolfe, E. E. Cummings, Edmund Wilson, James Thurber, Jack London, Tennessee Williams, Truman Capote, John Cheever, Conrad Aitken, Wolcott Gibbs, Stephen Crane, William Saroyan, Jack Kerouac, O. Henry, James Agee, Brendan Behan, Dylan Thomas, Edna St. Vincent Millay, James Jones, Irwin Shaw, Robert Ruark and Raymond Chandler got away with it, is no guarantee you will. Trust me on this.

If you get to work with an editor, protect your work but be willing to listen. The editor may know something. Before a shrewd editor suggested *Mein Kampf* as the title for the book he wrote while in jail, Adolf Hitler had planned to call it *Four-and-a-Half Years of Struggle Against Lies, Stupidity and Cowardice*. The words in the manuscript are yours and yours to protect within reason. But the best solution will be compromise. Asked by a London literary magazine to cut three lines from a five thousand word article, Henry James did so and returned it with a note saying, "I have performed the necessary butchery. Here is the bleeding corpse."

Writing is a skill. If it is born tiny, do not abandon it. It can be stroked and nursed into something big and healthy. It takes backbone. It takes skill, determination and belief in yourself. Be proud of your ability. Be true to your ability. It can't be done by talking about it or thinking about it. Writing has to be done. Most writers hate to write but love to have written.

Always write as best as you can. Always try to make it sing. If you can't, try to get it to hum a few bars.

". . . of making many books there is no end."

Ecclesiastes 12:12

After

As I write this, in the lovely Vancouver spring of 1995, I have been a working journalist for forty-four years. I have not earned a penny for anything but selling words since 1951. It's the only dodge for which I'm at all qualified.

I face the leering prospect of mandatory retirement at the age of sixty-five. (How the hell did that happen so suddenly?) But I'll keep writing for someone, somewhere. And I'll keep doing it until, with luck, I pitch face first into my computer screen after completing a readable column that will be published and piss off at least a few people.

I think I'm a good writer. I'm a good writer the same way that a journeyman carpenter with forty-four years experience is good. We have both taken a hard apprenticeship: we know our tools and materials and techniques. We know how to take rough materials — wood or words — and assemble them logically and attractively, give them a nice finishing polish and produce something useful.

I figure I have written somewhere between ten and twelve million words, most of which appeared in print and had a useful life for, oh, twenty-four hours, tops. You learn to live with the short shelf life.

If all that word-cranking had been assembled in a different format, it might have been forty or fifty novels. A couple of them might have hit and I might be sitting in the Bahamas, avoiding taxes.

But what the hell.

Somewhere, in a trunk in an attic, we all have a red bolo bat, a tartan toffee box from Jeanne Ferguson's Candy Store, Tenth and Granville, and a skate key on a loop of butcher's twine. And maybe a four-foot key chain from a 1940 zoot suit.

We marvel at the immediacy of the evening news on television. But we remember that Mr. Kelly concluded the evening news on radio by wishing us "a restful evening."

On second thought, we wish we had been there with a pocketful of cash when six Emily Carr originals sold for $50 each at a 1943 art auction.

We'd trade all the tofu sausages in the world for just one more of those heavy meat pies that Mrs. Egloff sold at Broadway and Hemlock.

We are not slaves to trendiness. We figure it's just another fettle of kitsch.

We never say we get a lot of rain. We say we get a lot of rainbows.

Marcel Proust began his seven-volume *Remembrance of Things Past* by recalling the sweet biscuits of his boyhood. This memoir began with the memory of a light on a post, a kind and useful one that could be leaned on, that scared the dark away, that pointed the way ahead. I can get into my car and drive out along Kingsway. If I squint my eyes, the streetlights still look like the moon on sticks. I have that much childish innocence left. Let me hold that thought.

like pink popcorn. It is summer in Vancouver when guys line up to buy lawn sprinklers at Canadian Tire. It is fall in Vancouver when Locarno Park crackles with fallen maple leaves. It is winter in Vancouver when the snow geese return to Boundary Bay. It is Christmas in Vancouver when the Parks Board rowboat hauls the big tree out to the fountain in Lost Lagoon.

There are trendy and calorically correct salads on the menu at White Spot. But the triple-O sauce remains unchanged, secret, tart and runny, and the dry cleaners' gratitude is undiminished.

The Lions Gate Bridge, our car-strangled spanner, is unchanged, since 1938, which is not reassuring. But it works on simple courtesy, when choked with morning traffic. People merge, people wave thanks. On one magic morning, I let a car pull ahead on the right. The window rolled down, and a feminine arm emerged, not clad in samite, not clutching Excalibur, but tanned and waving a red, red rose. I fell in love with the stranger.

One sees unchanging ugliness, squalor, in Pigeon Park. But there is also coarse dignity there, if one watches. When the old winos open a fresh bottle of screw-top bingo, they pour the first drops on the ground, no matter how thirsty they are. It is a benediction, a memory, a shared drink with those who have drunk themselves into the Beyond.

Stanley Park remains a wooded political battleground with car-haters, duck-feeders, whale-freers, tree-kissers. But where else in the world can a person drive through a rainforest, pass Robert Burns in bronze and be seven minutes from one's office? We are a special people, we Vancouverites.

We all own three umbrellas but none of us owns a hat.

Because we all listen to talk shows on the radio, we place telephone calls and, when answered, we ask, "Is that me?"

We are more proud of an old swizzle stick from the Arctic Club than a souvenir sweatshirt from a Rolling Stones concert.

We are resigned to the fact that we got our first sliced bread on July 19, 1937, that the last streetcar ran April 21, 1955, and that bread and transit have been pretty much screwed up ever since.

moving the Birks clock up and down Granville Street, but no matter where it is, people still agree to meet under it, a small assurance of permanence during change.

That same year the poet Pauline Johnson died. Her ashes were scattered on Siwash Rock. The offshore winds have rescattered the ashes in a tiny grove of trees near the water in Stanley Park; her spirit lives in the sparkle of fresh water that washes her memorial cairn. Assurance.

In 1889 Vancouver's first pay telephone was installed in the West End and the Nine O'clock Gun coughed for attention for the first time at Brockton Point. Every night, regular as, well, clockwork, the sound rumbles and rolls across the water, announcing a change of time but a continuance of habit.

I go to the produce market and contemplate vegetables laid out like trays of jewellery, ruby radishes, emerald Brussels sprouts, tiny pearl onions. And homely eggplants, looking like crates of bruised knees. They are all so tempting but impersonal. I remember the shy, smiling Chinese man who came to our house in his Model A truck with roll-down curtains on its sides. He brought fruit and vegetables to the door in bamboo baskets and left a gift of candied ginger at Christmas time.

I see a press release that says McGavin's has been selling bread in Vancouver for eighty years, a remarkable thing. But, also remarkable, I can remember when 4X bread was delivered by horse-drawn carts and that the horses, spooked by a streetcar's bell, occasionally bolted, spewing wrapped loaves and flying pies up Granville Street.

When I look at the new development on the north side of False Creek, I remember what a hellish industrial mess of ugly buildings and polluted air it once was. The yellow smoke that rolled up the slopes contributed to fogs of a porridge density that we don't get now. Those fogs choked us, but there was something magically eerie in hearing the muffled warning gong of an invisible streetcar, like the bell sound in Debussy's "The Engulfed Cathedral."

These things I hold true with assurance: It is spring in Vancouver when the cherry trees burst with clusters of blossoms

It's a small world but you wouldn't want to pay to have it painted.

We grow a day older every twenty-four hours. That's nature's cruelest law, but the little law-breaker that hides in all of us stays spitefully young. You can't make me eat my turnips. I bet I could still throw a lacrosse ball over the schoolhouse roof. I know I'm three steps slower going left or right, but in my mind, I am making the double-play.

After two marriages, I prefer to live alone. I have discovered that, at some point, bleak loneliness becomes valuable privacy, and privacy is freedom. I welcome visitors but avoid nesting women. You can recognize nesting women. They come to your door with twigs and bits of string in their beaks.

I'm not as nice as I once was. I am older, slower, less tolerant. I keep armed guards at all sides of my comfort zone.

I regard reaching the age of mandatory retirement as having been ambushed. Somebody snuck up, put a gun in my ribs and stole my working years.

But there is this thing called serenity which I learned about late in life. I still watch and treasure the sunsets from my balcony on the water in West Vancouver. In summer, they are slow, languorous, the horizon banded in strips of pastel, leaving a good night sky the colour of ripe peach flesh. In winter, they are quicker. There is furnace red and abrupt black. For the briefest while there are flickers of both, like reflections from a slowly turning roulette wheel.

It has been almost sixty years since I waded the sandy shallows of Kitsilano Beach, towing the wooden aircraft carrier my cousin Bert carved for me from a block of soft wood. Bert is gone, but the beach is still there and I can go there any time I want to, kick off my shoes and wade, buy a cardboard tub of sizzling fries, douse them with malt vinegar, watch another rapt kid tie a bunch of those tubs into a string of hand-towed barges. The thing is, if you have memories, it doesn't cost much to be happy in Vancouver. Inflation can't touch it.

There are changes and there are assurances in this town.

They opened the original Birks building in 1913. They keep

Free breakfast will be served every morning — broiled Bratwurst with triple-O sauce. Lena Horne will sing while you munch.

There will be a seawall, but there will be no joggers, cyclists, ghetto blasters, dogs or skateboarders.

Brilliant orange sunsets will occur hourly.

My kids and grandchildren will live a block away and come to visit once in a while.

Short people will be worshipped.

Living right on my block in heaven-on-earth will be W. C. Fields, Plato, Emily Bronte, Tom Robbins, Louis Armstrong, Julia Child, C. S. Forester, Dorothy Parker, Lord Byron, Alexander the Great, John F. Kennedy, Maurice Richard, Alexander Pope, my Grandfather Bill, Simon and Garfunkel, Goldie Hawn, Chief Dan George, Bronco Nagurski, Monty Python's Flying Circus, Giuseppe Verdi, Mike Royko, Jack Scott, Mother Teresa, Mary Queen of Scots, Job, Richard Harris, Robert Burns, Gilda Radner, Ernie Pyle, Harpo Marx, Tom T. Hall, Hannibal, Edith Piaf, Roderick Haig-Brown, Carl Yastrzemski, Hunter S. Thompson, Marian Anderson, Fred Astaire, the original Dave Brubeck Quartet, Johann Sebastian Bach, Dr. Bob and Bill W., Bruce Hutchison, Dylan Thomas, Gandhi, Jess Stacy, John Wayne, Winston Churchill, Rod Laver, Malcolm Lowry, Marco Polo, St. Francis of Assisi, W. O. Mitchell, W. A. C. Bennett, Nostradamus, Judy Holliday, Benjamin Spock, Daffy Duck, H. L. Mencken, Sigmund Freud, Abraham Lincoln, all the found-ins at the Cheers bar, McEyebrows and Lesley, Charles Dickens, Willie and Waylon, Stan Getz, Joey Smallwood, King Arthur, Stephen Leacock, Roy Henry Vickers and the Alfredo who invented Fettucini Alfredo. You will get to select your own neighbours. All of them will be eager to lend you their lawn mower.

I will write one column a week for the *Heavenly Herald* — if I feel like it.

To sum up . . .

Things change, things remain the same.

You win some, you lose some, and some go into extra innings.

Students will wear identical uniforms. Any student who wears a hat into a classroom will have to eat it.

There will be a cash penalty imposed on athletes every time they say "y'know" while being interviewed. The money collected will be used to build a linguistics school which will be mandatory for sports broadcasters.

After I get there I will be sixteen years old forever.

Your taxes, 3 per cent of your earnings, will be collected monthly at your door by Laurel and Hardy. If they make you laugh, you won't have to pay.

There will be no newscasts on television, but Kermit the Frog and Fozzie Bear will drop by every night to tell you what happened.

You will never have to make a left turn against traffic on heaven's highways, and car horns will play James Galway flute selections.

After a reasonable stay in heaven, I will meet K. T. Oslin and she will be mad for me.

Richard Nixon and Brian Mulroney will be there but they will be traffic bumps.

There will be tennis in heaven. There will be no double faults.

A proper heaven will have no place for mud, boiled turnips, junk mail, fern bars, New Year's Eve parties, seagulls, diesel buses, busy signals, toothaches, rock 'n roll drummers, Februaries, zits, ingrown toenails, high-fives, Big Macs, radical minorities, Los Angeles, Thomson newspapers, asphalt, grapefruit, tabloids, marketing boards, senators, sarcasm, rainy Saturdays, Velveeta cheese, parking meters, telephone surveys, polyester, accordion music, dandelions, lawyers, take-out chicken, designated hitters, obituary pages, pinkie rings, ear and chest hair, rattan furniture, knives, instant mashed potatoes, mauve Cadillacs, sideburns, television evangelists, synchronized swimming, one-way streets or Muzak.

When you get to heaven, your arrival will be celebrated by Woody Herman's 1945 brass section.

If you are dissatisfied with your body shape, you can chose a new one from a wide selection of attractive alternatives. I would like to look like a banjo.

Coleman Hawkins, Teddy Wilson and Buck Clayton will give free jam sessions every night. Lawrence Welk will be there, but he will be a plumber.

Radio announcers who say "Join Bob and I at 11 tonight" (as they all do), will be required to write on the blackboard one thousand times, "Me is illiterate."

In heaven it will cost $50,000 for a marriage license and seventy-five cents for a divorce.

There will be baseball, but it will be different. Any pitcher who hits a batter with a pitch will be required to stand perfectly still on the mound while the hitter throws his bat at him.

There will be football, too, but it will also be different. Players will be required to wear those silly paper hats that come in a Christmas cracker, which will put an end to spearing. Place kickers will have to do their work wearing shower clogs, which will create much hilarity and end a lot of boredom.

By definition, everyone will have a nice day in heaven-on-earth so there will be no need to say it. Anyone caught saying it will be permanently marooned in midstellar space where they can wish a million nice days to people who say "hopefully."

Politicians' terms will expire at midnight.

Heaven's tap water will taste like Courvoisier but have the effect of tap water,

Every New Democratic Government member will be admitted to heaven. But only half of them will retain the power of speech.

Protest groups will be given their say. But they will have to write their rants in perfect iambic pentameter and recite them in three-four time.

Cats in heaven will lose their snotty attitudes and learn to fetch. Dogs will eliminate all their body wastes in the form of mint-flavoured breath.

There will be no used car lots.

Rice will never stick to the bottom of the pot.

Sardine cans will have pop-tops.

There will be no weightlifters or hotdog skiers.

Chapter 16

In 1983, *U.S. Catholic Magazine* polled its readers about their vision of heaven. Very few of them responded. They may have suspected it was a trick question, loaded with divine implications. But those who did answer expressed a rather small vision, seeing heaven as a place where credit card limits and gas tanks never ran out.

Comedian Woody Allen, in one of his books, fretted about the afterlife. He wondered if you could get there from downtown, if it stays open late and if you can get your shirts back from the laundry in less than four days.

Because I don't really like to travel (I'm a bad packer and I'd hate to be stranded Up There for eternity without enough clean socks), I have been thinking that there's nothing wrong with heaven that a little relocation wouldn't help.

There has been enough wishful thinking and mooning about heaven-on-earth. Let's get on with it before real estate prices rise out of reach. Given a break by the construction unions, I could create it in six days. On the seventh day I would go fishing. It being heaven-on-earth I would, of course, catch my limit of big, sweet-fleshed trout. I haven't drawn up a budget but I do have the specs.

Heaven on earth will look like the Comox Valley but it would have salt water on three sides.

In heaven, an entire blueberry cheesecake will contain fourteen calories. Rye-Crisps, tofu, bean sprouts, canned peas and 2 per cent cottage cheese will be banned by the Divine Surgeon General.

186

'o's punched out. He wrote, "Dear Denny. I've been away in the States or you would have heard, before now, my opinion of your copy from Russia. It was by far the best stuff I've seen in recent years — a human touch instead of the usual ponderous political and economic abstractions that fill most newspapers. My congratulations." He signed it "Bruce" and then added in parentheses, "Hutchison," as if there might be confusion as to which Bruce he was.

The last time I saw Mr. Hutch was in 1991, at a private party held in Victoria Union Club to celebrate his ninetieth birthday. After a bang-up dinner, Mr. Hutch took over from the head table. Peering through a flickering candelabra at the darkened room, he identified all thirty of the guests by name and had a charming, witty remark for each of them.

Later I saw him waiting to be driven home, some gifts in one arm, the other hand holding one of those brightly coloured helium balloons that floated over his head. Canada's greatest journalist, at ninety, the birthday boy.

An enduring, endearing memory of a dear man.

"Nothing is simpler than to save the nation, or the world, in a square foot of black type. I have done it over and over again, thousands of times. Whenever I feel too old, tired and lazy to attempt anything more difficult, I save the world. It stubbornly refuses salvation, but newspaper proprietors, a naive and credulous breed, actually pay me for a job I could do in my sleep. Why, if I were a drinking man I could earn my wages dead drunk, as I have seen many abler men do six times a week in older times before the trade became respectable.

"After a few years' practice, you can finish the job in less than half an hour and leave the rest of the day for serious business or pleasure. Now, when my energies decay, it takes a little longer, sometimes a whole morning, merely to save Canada from its Government. Responsibility is the last refuge of decrepitude, the old man's home for broken journalists."

While he seldom mixed or socialized with them, Mr. Hutch was respected by other Canadian journalists. Robert Sheppard, the provincial affairs columnist for the Toronto *Globe and Mail*, a paper that rarely acknowledges the existence of others, certainly any others in a westerly direction, commented in 1990 about a four-part Hutchison series in the *Vancouver Sun*. "I have never met Mr. Hutchison though I have read several of his books about Canadian politics and prime ministers and have, like many other journalists, followed his career as probably the most revered of our number. The man who, for decades, told Western Canada about its national government . . .

"When I was a parliamentary reporter in The Globe's Ottawa bureau 10 or so years ago, he used to appear every year like an apparition. He would emerge from his Victoria garden and travel across the Rockies, dressed all in black, fedora and long trenchcoat, looking very much like the mad bomber in some Cold War cartoon."

And did I mention what a kind man he was? In 1989, I returned from my punishing tour of the crumbling Soviet Union to be greeted by what I felt was middle-management apathy over the project. But then I received a typed note from Mr. Hutch, with the

eyes, but by the brook, among the little poplars, there is shade and rest at noontime.

"The lean farmer follows the horses, trudging through the dust, his face black with dirt and sweat, and he knows only that he has plowed and sowed this ground and watched the little green shoots surge through the crust of spring and grow strong in the sunshine and soon he will feel the hard yellow grains in his hand. He knows only that he has laboured hard and produced good food that men need in their stomachs. Too much.

"Too much wheat, the clever men say, the men who have never felt plow handles, or the whip of the blizzard, or the dust and sweat in their eyes. We must cut down the wheat acreage, they say, as if it were just a chart on a piece of paper.

"But the farmer knows it is more than that. It is rich land, pregnant with fertility, urgent soil full of goodness, and its crop is solid substance, the ultimate wealth of the world, and to destroy it, to limit it, to waste it, violates laws far deeper than economics, not to be set down in chart or ledger."

Would it be presumptuous to point out that Mr. Hutch had learned his love of words by the age of eight, at a Victoria kindergarten run by Alice Carr, sister of the painter Emily, or that he was an expert horse rider by ten, and that he did not require post-secondary teaching?

Consider this opening to a 1967 magazine piece.

"I date the opening of my love story as Christmas Eve, 1910, in the cowtown of Merritt, British Columbia, when my father bought me a starving horse from Barnabas Blood, an Indian sub-chief of the lower Nicola reserve.

"I had not yet reached my tenth birthday but the scene of this purchase is clearer to me, and much more significant, than the news flowing across my editorial desk."

Did I mention that he had a sense of humour? Dry and self-deprecating it was. As in this:

"Anyone can write with solemn authority on public affairs, provided he knows little about them.

I've never won a journalism award, but in 1982 *Maclean's Magazine* did a two-page spread on me. Malcolm Gray wrote, "It's not great prose every time out, the grind of five columns a week sees to that, but occasionally across the bottom of page three, *The Vancouver Sun* has something rare in newspapers: good writing." He meant me. I'll settle for that as recognition.

I have worked for just two newspapers, but I have outlasted or fought to a tie ten managing editors and nine publishers/editors-in-chief. Most of them tolerated me; the majority liked my stuff. Most of them gave me that grandest of gifts, the freedom to write about anything I wanted to. Only one tried to bury my column and he damned near drove me into early retirement before we worked out an armed truce.

I have never thought of having a column as having power. I have thought of it as having privilege. It is a unique position to be able to display your opinions, likes and dislikes, every day and have people not only pay money and attention, but respond. That's a privilege that must be honoured and handled carefully.

I have never toppled a government or drummed out a corrupt public servant. I write to entertain; the hard news is on the other pages. But people stop me in the street and in the grocery store to tell me I have given them a good read from time to time, a few laughs, a few tears, and some of them say I helped get them over some rough spots without tearing out their keels.

Despite my efforts to screw it up, I've had a hell of a good life, more pure fun than anyone should expect from a career that kicks back a cheque every two weeks and pays the dentist bills and lets you decide every morning, on your own, what particular kind of widget you are going to invent that day.

My kids are grown up now. Unlike me, none of them has been in jail. No cop has ever knocked at my door with a complaint against one of them. I have six grandchildren — healthy, amusing, interesting grandchildren. The great thing about grandchildren is that you can tell them to go home if they start getting on your nerves.

By some uncharacteristic quirk of good sense, I turned down job offers that would have taken me to Toronto, Seattle or Atlanta. I realized that I couldn't take my beloved Coast Mountains with me. I'm still in the town I love. My office at the *Sun* was just four blocks from 1250 West Broadway, where I grew up in the late thirties. I like the narrowness of that circle of life. I can sit on my balcony on the West Vancouver waterfront and look out at the tethered deep sea freighters, turning on their anchor chains like range cattle facing into a blizzard. On summer Sunday nights I watch the cabin cruisers heading into harbour, sterns down, bows up, like fat little boys hurrying to be home before dark.

I have a card that my pal McEyebrows gave me for my sixty-fourth birthday. It has a pullaway sticker that says, "I've survived damned near everything." It's not a big exaggeration: scarlet fever, rheumatic fever, diabetes, heart attack, alcoholism, two divorces, a lot of bad decisions.

Every morning, when I take my first shot of insulin, I remind myself not to take a drink that day. The daily double discipline is life saving.

My life, which I steered into the bushes a few times, is serene and pretty much on track.

Then why do I still have that dream, two or three times a year, that dream of abject incompetence?

I'm in a strange town on assignment.

Sometimes it's a major sports event, sometimes a political convention. And I'm in a panic.

I'm walking strange streets, sweating. I can't find my hotel. It doesn't occur to me to call a taxi. I walk in and out of unfamiliar buildings, trying to get my bearings. People I don't know are sitting around drinking. They greet me and offer to buy me drinks, but they won't tell me where my hotel is. I have to get back to the hotel because I have to file my story. It's getting late and close to deadline. If I miss it, the people back at the paper will find out and say rotten things about me — that I can't hack it, that I'm not a real pro, that . . .

I wake up. My heart is pounding and my mouth is as dry as toilet paper. I lie there motionless for half a minute. Then I realize that I am at home. I look out the window and see the mast lights of a tug hauling a barge across the still water. Off to the left I can see the Lions Gate Bridge, lit up like the museum skeleton of an extinct beast.

I'm not lost. I haven't screwed up. They aren't talking about me. But I have to get up and walk the dream off. If I go right back to sleep, I'll pick up where I left off, looking for that damned hotel. When it's safe, I go back to sleep.

Or I'm back in the sports department of the *Victoria Times*, the young back-up left in charge while the sports editor is out of town. I've got a jumped-up copyboy and a ticked-off police reporter, temporarily reassigned, to help me. I have a pile of overnight wire copy on my desk, some pictures and three blank layout pages on my desk.

I have two and a half hours to fill those pages, to get all the copy edited, headlines written, pictures cropped and sized, and to get everything downstairs to the composing room or my section is going to be late. If I'm late, Jock the composing room foreman will cuss me and I'll get a nasty memo from the managing editor.

No problem. I've handled the pages dozens of time. It isn't that hard. All you have to do is get a rhythmic flow going. But this morning I can't get it going. I can't make decisions or concentrate. I feel panic. The clock is moving but the copy isn't. What the hell is happening. I'm going to blow it. I'm going to lose my job. And I wake up.

I'm in a hotel downtown. I'm interviewing a kid who has done some very noble thing for his mother. He has come into a pile of money somehow and he has chosen to spend it all on new furniture for his momma.

It will make a nice feel-good column and I know how to do those. As I ask the kid all the right questions, I am fishing through my pockets, trying to find a notebook or a piece of paper to record his answers. Every piece of paper I pull out is filled with notes from

other interviews. The kid is giving me great answers but I can't find space to write them down. And I realize that I can't remember anything he said two minutes ago. How bush-league is this?

The door opens and a number of hard-looking guys in expensive suits come in and sit down. They talk in whispers to the kid and he leaves. They ask me what he has said about the money and I tell them I can't remember and I haven't any notes. They move around me . . .

I'm awake again and pacing again and safe again and wondering what the hell that scene was all about.

Well, what is it about? Paranoia? Self-doubt? Insecurity? That bit of Brie I ate before bed? Bad conscience? Alcoholic flashback? Beats the hell out of me.

The best answer I can come up with is that I'm getting night-rate messages from my Higher Power that I might not pay attention to during the distractions of daytime.

The message might be interpreted as a warning to remember that serenity and sobriety are handed out of a day-to-day basis. You can't buy them in case lots and store them away. And the supply is cancellable without notice.

In those first heart-pounding minutes of wakefulness, I resent the hyperbole of the message. Hey, I've been sober a long time, my dues are paid up. Cut me some slack. Let me sleep.

But I post the message. I know I'm at risk so I pay attention. I have to.